Cambridge Elements

Elements in Applied Evolutionary Science
edited by
David F. Bjorklund
Florida Atlantic University

STRENGTHS AND WEAKNESSES OF TWO THEORIES FOR EXPLAINING 15 UNIVERSAL SEX DIFFERENCES IN COGNITION AND BEHAVIOR

Lee Ellis
University of Malaya

Shaftesbury Road, Cambridge CB2 8EA, United Kingdom

One Liberty Plaza, 20th Floor, New York, NY 10006, USA

477 Williamstown Road, Port Melbourne, VIC 3207, Australia

314–321, 3rd Floor, Plot 3, Splendor Forum, Jasola District Centre, New Delhi – 110025, India

103 Penang Road, #05–06/07, Visioncrest Commercial, Singapore 238467

Cambridge University Press is part of Cambridge University Press & Assessment, a department of the University of Cambridge.

We share the University's mission to contribute to society through the pursuit of education, learning and research at the highest international levels of excellence.

www.cambridge.org
Information on this title: www.cambridge.org/9781009581004

DOI: 10.1017/9781009581028

© Lee Ellis 2025

This publication is in copyright. Subject to statutory exception and to the provisions of relevant collective licensing agreements, no reproduction of any part may take place without the written permission of Cambridge University Press & Assessment.

When citing this work, please include a reference to the DOI 10.1017/9781009581028

First published 2025

A catalogue record for this publication is available from the British Library

ISBN 978-1-009-58100-4 Hardback
ISBN 978-1-009-58104-2 Paperback
ISSN 2752-9428 (online)
ISSN 2752-941X (print)

Cambridge University Press & Assessment has no responsibility for the persistence or accuracy of URLs for external or third-party internet websites referred to in this publication and does not guarantee that any content on such websites is, or will remain, accurate or appropriate.

For EU product safety concerns, contact us at Calle de José Abascal, 56, 1°, 28003 Madrid, Spain, or email eugpsr@cambridge.org

Strengths and Weaknesses of Two Theories for Explaining 15 Universal Sex Differences in Cognition and Behavior

Elements in Applied Evolutionary Science

DOI: 10.1017/9781009581028
First published online: August 2025

Lee Ellis
University of Malaya

Author for correspondence: Lee Ellis, lee.ellis@hotmail.com

Abstract: Social role theory and evolutionary neuroandrogenic (ENA) theory are compared regarding how well they can explain 15 cognitive and behavioral sex differences that appear to be present in all human cultures. In essence, social role theory argues that, except for males being larger and more muscular and only females being able to bear children, cognitive and behavioral differences between the sexes result from sociocultural training and expectations. On the other hand, ENA theory attributes sex differences in cognition and behavior to evolved differential exposure of male and female brains to sex hormones, especially testosterone. The existence of 15 nearly certain universal sex differences in cognitive and behavioral traits was documented in a recently published book based on findings from over 40,000 empirical studies. This Element documents that, while both theories have explanatory power, ENA theory surpasses social role theory in explaining the universality of most of the 15 traits.

Keywords: universal sex differences, cognition, behavior, social role theory, evolutionary neuroandrogenic theory

© Lee Ellis 2025

ISBNs: 9781009581004 (HB), 9781009581042 (PB), 9781009581028 (OC)
ISSNs: 2752-9428 (online), 2752-941X (print)

Contents

1 Methodology   1

2 Two Theories for Explaining Universal Sex Differences   7

3 Applying Social Role Theory and ENA Theory to Each One of the 15 Nearly Certain Universal Sex Differences in Cognition and Behavior   19

4 Discussion   44

5 Conclusions   49

   References   52

Universal Cognitive and Behavioral Sex Differences

For over a century, scientists have empirically documented the existence of many average sex differences in how people think and behave (reviews: Archer, 2019; Ellis et al., 2008; Geary, 2021; Halpern, 2000; Kimura, 2000; Mealey, 2000). Because most studies of sex differences limit their samples to a single country, it is difficult to know if any identified sex difference is culturally specific or culturally universal.

Given the importance of human learning and the fact that cultures vary greatly in how males and females are treated, most social scientists believe that there are few if any cognitive and behavior patterns for which the sexes would differ *in the same way* throughout the world (Horowitz et al., 2014; Sanderson & Ellis, 1992). In other words, while males may exhibit a particular trait more than females do in one culture, it is likely that the opposite pattern (or at least no sex difference at all) exists in other cultures.

Until now, the closest scientists have gotten to empirically documenting the existence of universal sex differences (USDs) has come in two forms: One is multinational surveys in which consortiums of researchers administer the same questionnaire (except for the language utilized) to samples of males and females living in a variety of diverse countries. Based on self-reports, these studies have provided surprising evidence that quite a few USDs could in fact exist, especially when it comes to occupational interests and preferences for mates (Buss, 1989; Lippa, 2009, 2010; Okami & Shackelford, 2001; Schmitt et al., 2008; Schwartz & Rubel, 2005; Archer, 2019; Stoet & Geary, 2020).

Another approach to documenting the existence of USDs involves conducting extensive literature reviews and meta-analyses. Recent examples include research covering sex differences in traits involving depression (Salk et al., 2017), childhood toy preferences (Davis & Hines, 2020), food preferences (Modlinska et al., 2020), insomnia (Zeng et al., 2020), and suicidal behavior (Miranda-Mendizabal et al., 2019). In the case of meta-analyses, researchers often derive a final statistical estimate of the degree to which males and females differ (usually in the form of a d or *effect size*). While certainly pertinent to USD research, literature reviews and meta-analyses rarely keep track of how many different countries were sampled.

As explained next, the present inquiry utilizes a third approach to identifying USDs. It involves tabulating findings from as many research reports as can be found regarding sex differences while keeping track of the countries sampled as well as also including literature reviews and meta-analyses.

1 Methodology

Recently, three colleagues and I published a four-volume book in which over 40,000 studies were referenced, all having to do with sex differences. Citations to these studies were organized into roughly 6,000 tables, with each table pertaining to a different variable.

The book's first three volumes focused on (a) basic biological traits (Ellis et al., 2024a), (b) cognitive traits (Ellis et al., 2024b), and (c) behavioral traits (Ellis et al., 2024c), respectively. In the book's fourth volume, the primary objective was to tabulate the number of studies cited in each one of the roughly 6,000 tables located throughout the first three volumes with at least ten studies cited. This allowed us to identify the most promising USDs by looking for tables in which there was strong agreement as to the nature of specific sex differences.

We were especially interested in making our review as international in scope as possible. Therefore, studies cited within each table were organized according to the countries from which their samples were drawn. Furthermore, being cognizant of the fact that most behavioral and social science research is conducted in so-called *WEIRD* (i.e., Western, Educated, Industrialized, Rich, and Democratic) *countries*, we made special effort to include as many non-WEIRD countries as could be located. Despite these efforts, the bulk of research findings still ended up coming from WEIRD country samples.

Quite a few of the studies cited in the book's first three volumes were based on samples drawn from two or more countries. In these multinational studies, if the statistical significance was reported for each country separately (always using a $p < 0.05$ cutoff), we made individual citations to each country. Otherwise, when just a single statistically significant sex difference was reported for all of the countries sampled, the results were reported under a category termed *Multiple Countries*.

As a way of cross-checking findings, we also included citations to literature reviews and meta-analyses. Their conclusions were cited following a special header named *Overview*.

The book's final volume (Ellis et al., 2024d) is particularly relevant to the present series Element. As already noted, the main purpose of our final volume was to condense information contained in the 6,000+ tables presented throughout the book's first three volumes. This involved counting the number of studies in each table, along with the number of countries cited and the number of literature reviews and meta-analyses. Ultimately, in the book's final volume, our focus was on the tables throughout Volumes I, II, and III that contain *at least ten citations* (excluding citations to literature reviews and meta-analyses). In this way, we were able to look for consistencies in the findings of all tables containing at least ten citations.

One result of compiling information for the tables appearing throughout Volume IV was the identification of 131 sex difference of a cognitive nature (documented in Volume II) and 144 sex differences pertaining to behavior (documented in Volume III) for which there were at least ten pertinent findings, all pointing in essentially the same direction (i.e., either males exhibited the trait more or females did). My coauthors and I identified these 275 sex difference variables as being *probable USDs*. No attempt will be made here to identify these variables; interested readers can find them described in pages 80–300 of Volume IV.

The focus of the present Element will be confined to just 15 of the 275 variables. What makes these 15 variables special is that in more than 100 studies (rather than just 10) all indicated that there were consistent sex differences. A listing of these fifteen variables appear in the first column of Table 1. They are in descending order according to the total number of studies located (shown in Column 3). Henceforth, I will refer to these variables as *nearly certain USDs*. In addition to listing these fifteen variables, Table 1 provides the following items of information:

Column 2. The sex exhibiting each one of the fifteen traits the most

Column 3. The total number of studies that were supportive of a particular sex difference divided by the total number of studies

Column 4. The percentage of support (apart from any qualifying comments)

Column 5. The number of countries sampled (with numbers in parentheses identifying how many studies of multiple countries were also sampled)

Column 6. The number of literature reviews and/or meta-analyses (all of which were found to agree with our counts of the individual studies regarding which sex exhibited the trait the most)

Column 7. Table numbers in our book's first three volumes for readers interested in examining the actual 100+ citations bearing on each nearly certain USD.

The last two (slightly shaded) columns in Table 1 pertain to how well social role theory and ENA theory do in explaining why each one of the fifteen USDs is found in all human societies. The following four notations are used: An "x" means that either of the two theories offers no plausible explanation for a particular USD. A single checkmark means that a theory provides a plausible way of explaining why a particular sex difference might be found throughout the world, although no empirical evidence bolstering this line of reasoning was located. When two checkmarks appear, a theory not only offers a plausible explanation for a particular USD, at least one line of empirical evidence supporting this explanation was also found. In the case of three checkmarks appearing in Table 1, two or more lines of empirical support for a theoretical explanation were located.

A final methodological issue has to do with the statistical significance of the studies pertaining to each of the fifteen variables listed in Table 1. As already noted, $p < 0.05$ was the accepted cutoff used throughout our book to identify sex

Table 1 The fifteen nearly certain cognitive and behavioral USDs

Variable (1)	Sex Highest for Each Trait (2)	Proportion of Findings Supportive (3)	% Support (4)	Number of Countries Sampled (5)	Literature Reviews and Meta-analyses* (6)	Table Cited (7)	Explanatory Power	
							Social Role Theory (8)	ENA Theory (9)
1. Earnings/salaries for workers	Male	579/587	98.0	47 (58)	0 Review, 3 Metas	20.3.1.1	✓✓✓	✓✓✓
2. Performing routine indoor household chores	Female	334/337	99.1	31 (41)	11 Reviews, 0 Metas	20.3.3.1	x	✓✓
3. Self-reported criminal/delinquent offending in general	Male	227/233	97.4	46 (7)	0 Reviews, 0 Metas	19.1.2.1	✓	✓✓✓
4. Officially identified criminal offending in general	Male	189/191	99.0	30 (10)	2 Reviews, 1 Meta	19.1.1.1	✓✓	✓✓✓
5. Engaging in physical exercise	Male	142/149	95.3	18 (4)	2 Reviews 0 Metas	16.3.2.2	x	✓✓✓

6. Achieving prominence in one's occupational field	Male	146/148	98.6	22 (20)	0 Reviews, 0 Metas	20.4.3.4	✓	✓✓✓
7. Accidental injuries and fatalities in general	Male	130/134	97.0	17 (11)	1 Review, 1 Meta	5.2.1.1	✓	✓✓✓
8. Holding elected political office	Male	127/129	98.4	22 (22)	0 Reviews, 0 Metas	20.2.7.51	✓	✓✓
9. Attention deficit hyperactivity disorder	Male	124/126	98.4	18	2 Reviews, 3 Metas	14.4.8.1	x	✓✓
10. Conduct disorder	Male	126/131	96.2	19 (1)	8 Reviews, 0 Metas	14.4.3.1	x	✓✓
11. Participation in paid workforce in general (among adults)	Male	112/116	96.6	40 (20)	0 Reviews, 0 Metas	20.2.1.1	✓✓✓	✓✓
12. Risk-taking (recklessness) in general	Male	104/109	95.4	14 (2)	3 Reviews, 2 Metas	16.2.3.1	✓✓	✓✓✓

Table 1 (cont.)

Variable (1)	Sex Highest for Each Trait (2)	Proportion of Findings Supportive (3)	% Support (4)	Number of Countries Sampled (5)	Literature Reviews and Meta-analyses* (6)	Table Cited (7)	Explanatory Power	
							Social Role Theory (8)	ENA Theory (9)
13. Preference for a mate with resources (wealth, high income)	Female	104/107	97.2	27 (12)	2 Reviews, 1 Meta	15.6.5.9	✓	✓✓
14. Majoring in the physical sciences or engineering	Male	98/102	96.1	11 (5)	0 Reviews, 0 Metas	20.1.4.26	x	✓✓
15. Homicide perpetration	Male	101/101	100.0	25 (22)	0 Reviews, 0 Metas	19.1.1.3	✓✓	✓✓✓

* All literature reviews and meta-analyses concurred with the conclusions shown in the second column regarding which sex displayed each trait listed in the first column.

x – silent
✓ – plausible arguments without supportive independent empirical evidence
✓✓ – some supportive independent empirical evidence
✓✓✓ – substantial supportive independent empirical evidence

differences that were statistically significant. Consequently, about one out of every twenty studies will be identified as not being significantly different when they are different. Of course, relatively small sample size is the most common reason for real differences not being statistically significant. In this regard, one should bear in mind that many of the statistically significant studies are significant well beyond the 0.05 level, for example, at the 0.01 or even the 0.001 levels. Therefore, even though several of the fifteen sex difference variables listed in Table 1 contain a few finding that fell short of the 0.05 level of significance, they should not be considered a serious challenge to conclusion that each of these fifteen sex differences are "real." This conclusion is reinforced by the fact that all the variables listed in Table 1 for which literature reviews and meta-analyses were located (shown in Column 6) agreed that significant sex differences exist.

2 Two Theories for Explaining Universal Sex Differences

Given the vast diversity in human cultures and the obvious role played by learning in human thought and behavior, it is reasonable to believe that cognitive and behavioral sex differences are highly influenced by cultural factors. On the other hand, because human thoughts and actions are controlled by the brain, and sex differences in the brain have been extensively documented (Zaidi, 2010; review: Ellis et al., 2024a, pp. 330–474), it is not unreasonable to believe that some cognitive and behavioral sex differences might exist in all cultures. Furthermore, many of the average sex differences in brain structures and functioning have been shown to be under substantial genetic control (Ngun et al., 2011; Ratnu et al., 2017). These genetic influences are achieved in part through their abilities to regulate and interact with various sex hormonal regimens (Tahira et al., 2019). Such evidence leads one to infer that genes have evolved in humans (as well as other life forms) to ensure *their* (not our) virtual immortality (Dawkins, 2006).

So, to what extent are sex differences in thought and behavior a reflection of our desires to conform to cultural expectations or to our evolved genetic programming? If both are involved, how do they impinge upon sex differences in cognition and behavior? As this section will show, two scientific theories have addressed these types of questions and come to substantially different conclusions. After describing these two theories, I will show how the fifteen sex differences described in Table 1 can shed light on the strengths and weaknesses of both theories.

The two theories to be described are *social role theory* and the *evolutionary neuroandrogenic (ENA) theory*. After describing each theory, I will focus on how well each theory explains each one of the fifteen the USDs listed in Table 1.

Before describing each theory, let me mention that one other theoretical proposal has been offered to explain the existence of USDs. It is Fausto-Sterling's (1992) *founder effect theory*. This theory argues that USDs in behavior exist because they arose in primordial times and have been "faithfully passed down a thousand times over" throughout the course of human evolution (p. 199). Unfortunately, this theory provides no guidance for assessing its testability. In other words, no specific cognitive or behavioral sex differences were named and the phrase "faithfully passed down a thousand times over" does not predict which sex differences should and should not be passed down. For this reason, I will not attempt to include the founder effect theory in the present analysis.

2.1 Social Role Theory

The idea that sex differences in behavior are due to social role training and cultural expectations can be traced back to the first half of the twentieth Century (Mead, 1935, 1949). Not until the latter half of this past century was this perspective formalized into an actual scientific theory under the name of *social role theory* (Eagly, 1987, 1997; Eagly & Wood, 1991). As the twentieth century drew to a close, however, Eagly and Wood began using different names to identify their theory. Specifically, in 1999, they referred to it as *social structural theory* (Eagly & Wood, 1999). A few years later, the term *biosocial role theory* was used (Eagly & Wood, 2005, 2012) and changed most recently to *biosocial constructionist theory* (Eagly & Wood, 2013, p. 11).

Based on personal correspondence with Dr. Alice Eagly (December 3, 2023), I was able to determine that these alternate names all refer to essentially the same theory that she first advocated in the 1980s under the name of *social role theory*. The only difference between *social role theory* and the more recently used terms is that the latter names tend to emphasize that certain biological factors can influence cognitive and behavioral sex differences that may be universal. The nature of these biological factors is specified further.

To decide which term to use throughout the present report when referring to Eagly and Wood's theory, in 2024, I conducted a search on Google Scholar for each one of the four theory names that have been used. Doing so resulted in the following numbers:

Social role theory – 19,300 hits
Social structural theory – 1,300 hits
Biosocial role theory – 27 hits
Biosocial constructionist theory – 36 hits.

These numbers clearly show that the theory's original name – that of *social role theory* – has been used much more often in scientific publications than any of the other three names. Parenthetically, in a kind email exchange with me,

Dr. Eagly stated her own preference for *social role theory* as the single-best term to use. My efforts to contact Dr. Windy Wood, Eagly's frequent coauthor, on this matter were not successful.

At the heart of social role theory is the idea that each culture prescribes how males and females are expected (or stereotyped) to behave. Then, as children are socialized by parents, teachers, and others, most boys and girls gradually come to accept their endogenous sex or gender as reflecting their emerging positions in society. Based on this acceptance, boys and girls begin to emulate the sex-appropriate cultural stereotypes that they associate with being males and females (Bussey & Bandura, 1999; Eagly, 1987). Each culture's stereotypes about sex differences in behavior, called *sex roles*, end up being passed down from one generation to the next with very few alterations.

There is an important caveat to this description of social role theory. This caveat is used to help explain why certain cognitive and behavioral sex differences can end up being culturally universal. It stated that cultural influences on cognitive and behavioral traits must always work within certain biological constraints. Specifically, the fact that, as adults, males tend to be taller and physically stronger, plus the fact that only females can bear offspring, has biasing effects on sex differences in behavior (Eagly & Wood, 2013; Wood & Eagly, 2012). For example, because of these three biological sex differences, males will be more likely to learn and be reinforced by their cultures for exhibiting patterns of behavior that complements their greater size and strength. Similarly, females will be more likely to learn attitudes and behaviors that support their abilities to bear offspring.

Overall, were it not for the fact that males are taller and stronger and only females can bear children, social role theory predicts that all average sex differences in thoughts and behavior are the result of cultural factors. These cultural influences include such variables as dress codes, laws promoting or discouraging sex discrimination, and a variety of restrictions made on one sex or the other in hiring and other economic transactions. To explain USDs, social role theory asserts that, due to the greater average size and strength and to the fact that only females can give birth, many sex differences in behavior will be similar (Wood & Eagly, 2012).

To illustrate this point, social role theory predicts that, in all cultures, males will be more likely than females to take up occupations involving strenuous labor and frequent bursts of energy, while females will be more likely to gravitate toward providing childcare (Eagly & Wood, 2012, p. 465). Furthermore, given men's greater physical strength, social role theory has even been used to predict that males will be more aggressive and involved in warfare throughout the world (Eagly & Wood, 2012, p. 465). I will revisit this argument when dealing with homicidal behavior being a USD (Variable 15).

In one of their articles, Wood and Eagly (2002, p. 702) offered the following summary of their theory: "Physical sex differences, in interaction with social and ecological conditions, influence the roles held by men and women because certain activities are more efficiently accomplished by one sex. It can thus be easier for one sex than the other to perform certain activities of daily life under given conditions." More recently, a team of researchers summarized social role theory as follows: "Men and women are differently distributed into social roles because of humans' evolved physical sex differences by which men are stronger, larger, and faster than women and women gestate and nurse children. Because of these physical differences, certain activities are more efficiently accomplished by one sex or the other, depending on each society's circumstances and culture" (Steinmetz et al., 2014, p. 52).

Elsewhere, Eagly and Wood (2005, p. 282) state that their theory leads to the expectation of behavioral sex differences "across societies in the activities most closely enabled or constrained by sex-typed physical attributes and reproductive activities." Overall, social role theory predicts that there will be few if any USDs *unless* those traits are linked to males being taller and stronger and/or only females being able to bear and nurse offspring.

To provide clarity regarding social role theory, Wood and Eagly (2012) have offered graphic models of the main processes involved in their theory. In a subsequent section of this Element, this graphic model will be presented and discussed.

2.2 Evolutionary Neuroandrogenic Theory

The other theory for explaining why some sex differences would be found in all societies is known as ENA theory (Ellis, 2003, 2011). As its name implies, this theory combines evolutionary concepts with evidence that male sex hormones, particularly testosterone, affect brain functioning in ways that often results in males and females thinking and behaving differently on average. One can say that the theory's evolutionary component addresses the question of *why* sex differences exist, while the neuroandrogenic component specifies *how* sex differences materialize. The "why" issues of the theory are sometimes known as *ultimate influences*, whereas the "how" issues are called *proximate influences* (Scott-Phillips et al., 2011). Each of these two theoretical components is described in greater detail next.

2.2.1 The Evolutionary Foundation

About a century and a half ago, Charles Darwin (1871) proposed the concept of *sexual selection* to refer to a special type of natural selection. The primary difference between these two evolutionary concepts is as follows: *Natural selection* involves forces that impinge from outside of a group of organisms that can affect their ability to reproduce (e.g., food availability and predation risks). *Sexual selection*, on the other hand, occurs *between* members of sexually reproducing species. Examples of sexually selected traits are preferences and actions taken by members of one sex toward a prospective mate, along with responses to actions by members of the opposite sex. Such preferences and actions can often affect how many offspring each sex is able to leave in subsequent generations (Fisher, 1930; Trivers, 1972). For instance, by possessing a trait that enhances a male's sexual attractiveness to females, the trait is being subjected to sexual selection. Sexually selected traits can be physical, cognitive, or behavioral in nature, but they must all have some underlying genetic foundation (Fromonteil et al., 2023). Examples of sexual selection include both physical and behavioral traits (e.g., size and coordination) that males use to help ward off rival males from mating opportunities, or traits exhibited by females that males find sexually attractive (Daly, 2017). Even the care given by males or females to their offspring can be seen as having been subjected to sexual selection (Puts, 2016; Wilson et al., 2017).

In Darwinian terms, because of the lengthy gestational period involved in producing an offspring, females should be more cautious than males when it comes to mating. Thus, the sexual selection component of Darwin's theory can help to explain several sex differences in behavior, not only in humans (Buss, 2007; Del Giudice, 2023; Geary, 2021; Okami & Shackelford, 2001; Puts et al., 2012) but in other species as well (Key & Ross, 1999; Petersen & Higham, 2020; Schuett et al., 2010).

To provide a specific example, consider promiscuity. Theoretically, males who desire sex with numerous sex partners, and at least occasionally act on those desires, are likely to leave more copies of their genes in subsequent generations than males who choose to be sexually exclusive to just a single mating partner (Schmitt, 2003; Geher & Kaufman, 2013; Janicke et al., 2016). This would be especially true for earlier periods in human history before the advent of modern contraception and the widespread availability of abortion. On the other hand, females with equally strong desires for multiple sex partners would rarely have a reproductive advantage over females who are content with having just one sex partner (Buss & Schmitt, 2017).

From the perspective of sexual selection, sex differences are rooted in recognizing that, among mammals, only females can gestate offspring. One consequence is that, once a female becomes pregnant, her reproductive potential depends on successfully gestating each fetus she is carries and then nurturing the offspring after birth. Males, however, have fewer constraints on their abilities to reproduce since their investment is limited to the insemination process.

Another example of how sexual selection theory has been used to explain sex differences involves physical strength and the ability to spatially navigate. Both traits are likely to have helped humans track, chase, and throw lethal projectiles at prey (Geary, 2021; Kolakowski & Malina, 1974). Theoretically, males would have been favored for these activities more than females because gestating and breastfeeding offspring restricts the time and effort females can devote to effectively tracking and killing wild game (Kordsmeyer et al., 2018; Marlowe, 2007; Trivers, 1976).

Overall, Darwin's (1871) theory of sexual selection is an extension of his theory of natural section, and has provided a springboard for many hypotheses having to do with how males and females, on average, might differ. In most cases, the theory implies that a substantial number of USDs should exist (Fromonteil et al., 2023). One proponent of sexual selection theory argued as follows: "If a sex difference occurs consistently, despite all the variations in learning and socialization practices that occur across cultures, then . . . an innate predisposition is probably showing through all the cultural 'noise'" (Lippa, 2002, p. 116).

2.2.2 Augmenting Sexual Selection with Neurohormonal Variables

Sexual selection theory has achieved impressive success in offering accounts for *why* a variety of sex differences in various cognitive and behavioral traits might exist (Clutton-Brock & Vincent, 1991; Jones & Ratterman, 2009; Lüpold, Manier et al., 2016). Nevertheless, this theory is limited from the fact that, because evolved traits of a cognitive or behavioral nature are rarely fossilized, direct evidence of their evolution is all but impossible to obtain.

Given the difficulties involved in directly testing sexual selection theory, critics have pointed out that much of the supportive evidence has involved searching for sex differences in traits that happen to conform to the theory, while ignoring many other sex differences that do not conform (Hankin, 2013). This point was made by Eagly and Wood (1999, p. 420) in their criticism of sexual selection theory as follows: "It is far too easy to make up sensible stories about how these differences might be products of sex-differentiated evolved tendencies or the differing placement of women and men in the social structure."

Scientific theories can often be enhanced by incorporating conceptual components that make them more testable. Of course, adding concepts usually involves trade-offs between simplicity and greater complexity; obviously, all else being equal, simpler theories are better than complex theories. In other words, if adding more conceptual components to a theory gives it greater explanatory power, the resulting increase in complexity can often be justified

(Murphy & Medin, 1985). To illustrate this point, Darwin's theory was expanded in the early part of the twentieth century with what has come to be known as the *Modern Synthesis*. This synthesis involved adding genetic concepts to Darwin's original theory, concepts that were nonexistent during Darwin's life (Huxley, 1942; Pinker, 2002). Today, scientists can use this gene-enhanced version of Darwin's theory to help account for many more biological phenomena than was possible with his original theory (Kutschera & Niklas, 2004; Jobling & Tyler-Smith, 2019).

While many genes may play a role in producing sex differences, the most crucial genes reside on the two so-called sex chromosomes, especially the Y chromosome (Charlesworth, 1991; Iannuzzi et al., 2023; Roldan & Gomendio, 1999). Over the past several decades, a great deal has been learned about how genes help to guide sexual development, including sexual differentiation of the brain (Jacobs, 1996; Ryan, 2021). Considerable evidence suggests that the brain is sexually dimorphic both anatomically and functionally in numerous ways (review: Ellis et al., 2024a, pp. 330–474). Most of the differentiation of the brain is the result of both prenatal and postpubertal exposure to various sex hormones, particularly testosterone (Celec et al., 2015; Herbert, 2015; Jašarević et al., 2012; Negri-Cesi et al., 2004). In other words, many of the genes that result in the production of male-typical amounts of testosterone among males have accumulated mainly (but not exclusively) on the Y chromosome. Since only males carry this chromosome, its genes virtually ensure that males will produce more testosterone than females do (Knickmeyer & Baron-Cohen, 2006). Testosterone is primarily produced outside of the nervous system (especially by the testes). Some externally produced testosterone is able to penetrate the brain, both prenatally and following puberty by passing through the so-called *blood–brain barrier* (Kopsida et al., 2009; Savic et al., 2017). In this way, testosterone seems to have multiple influences on how organisms (including humans) think and behave.

Overall, due to genes affecting the production of testosterone and the ability of testosterone to affect brain functioning, males and females exhibit a variety of average differences in thought and behavior (e.g., Hooven 2021; Manning & Taylor, 2001; Martel, 2013; Sinervo et al., 2000). This means that one can add neurohormonal concepts to Darwinian theory. By doing so, his theory can be tested in many ways than was the case prior to the Modern Synthesis and even more after the addition of neurohormonal concepts (Jašarević et al., 2012).

I have proposed calling this neurohormonal version of Darwin's gene-enhanced theory the *evolutionary neuroandrogenic* (*ENA*) *theory* (Ellis, 2003, 2006, 2011). In essence, ENA theory supplements the Modern Synthesis version of Darwinian theory with additional variables having to do with testosterone and brain functioning. And, because the brains of males and females are exposed to differing amounts of testosterone, ENA theory predicts the existence of sex differences in cognitive and behavioral traits.

Overall, ENA theory asserts that the main driver of sex differences in cognition and behavior involves the evolution of hormones (testosterone in particular) that also affects sex differences in traits that make males more attractive to females. As stated by Malisa Hines (2004, p. 65), "[t]he existence of sex differences in behavior implies the existence of sex differences in the brain because the brain provides the basis for all behavior." I would add that her statement holds true not only for behavior but also for cognitive traits such as emotions, reasoning, interests, preferences, and a variety of physical traits.

To conceptualize average sex differences in exposure to testosterone, readers can refer to Figure 1. This graph provides an estimate of how this exposure varies from conception to the end of life. As one can see, there are major sex differences throughout life in testosterone levels except in the case of childhood, when differences tend to be minor.

Two qualifying comments are worth making regarding this graph: First, most of the *permanent* sexing of the brain occurs prenatally, whereas most of testosterone's so-called *activational effects* occurs following the onset of puberty (Auyeung et al., 2013).

Second, Figure 1 provides a rough indication of sex differences in the production of testosterone throughout life, including the levels that penetrate the brain (Celec et al., 2015; Gooren, 2007). One can see that by the time males are born, their average exposure to testosterone is much greater than is the case

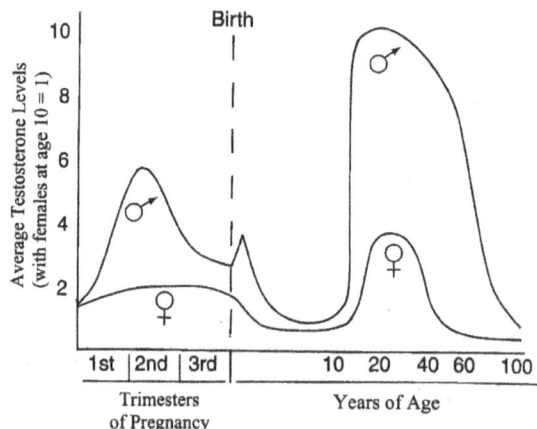

Figure 1 Testosterone levels of human males and females from conception through old age.

for the average female. Following puberty, male exposure to testosterone also greatly surpasses that of the average female (for a summary of the evidence regarding sex differences in testosterone exposure, see Ellis et al., 2024a, pp. 223–226). Research has indicated that the more the brain is exposed to testosterone, the more it is masculinized (i.e., made more male-typical), and the more masculinized the brain, the more male-typical cognition and behavior will usually be throughout life (Baron-Cohen et al., 2006; Pfaf et al., 2018).

Scientific evidence regarding the effects of testosterone on brain functioning is extensive (Mehta et al., 2008; Volman et al., 2011; Welker et al., 2015). While investigations are still ongoing, findings have already shown that, when neurological levels of testosterone are high (i.e., in the male-typical range), key reward-sensitive areas of the brain often promote dopamine production. Dopamine is a neurotransmitter that is often associated with feelings of accomplishment and keen motivation to socially compete (Breuning, 2018; Smith et al., 2013). Also, dopamine in the brain often promotes whatever types of thoughts and behaviors individuals are engaged in at the time of exposure (Campbell et al., 2010; Eisenegger et al., 2017). Many other neurological changes also occur in response to testosterone, changes that are likely to have numerous influences on cognition and behavior (Davis & Pfaff, 2014; Geary, 2019; Henriques-Neto et al., 2023).

According to ENA theory, sex differences in many cognitive and behavioral traits have evolved because they have a tendency to help males and females obtain mating opportunities, thereby contributing to the representation of their genes in future generations. Regarding neurology, sex differences in brain functioning have evolved because many of these differences promote cognitive and behavioral traits that have been sexually selected. It is only a slight oversimplification to say that, for every USD in cognition and behavior that exists, ENA theory predicts that *both* sexual selection and brain exposure to testosterone are involved (Ellis, 2011).

An important issue to address regarding ENA theory has to do with measuring testosterone exposure. While the theory states that brain exposure is a central feature, in fact, this is nearly impossible to empirically document without risking damage to the brain. Therefore, most researchers who are interested in the effects of testosterone on brain functioning end up relying on peripheral measures (i.e., measures outside of the brain itself such as the amniotic fluid, blood, or saliva). If these measures are obtained before birth, they are known as *prenatal levels*; if they are assessed at any time thereafter, especially following puberty, they are usually known as *circulating levels*. Most measures of circulating testosterone are from the blood or saliva. However, testosterone levels fluctuate throughout the day, with the highest and most stable levels occurring soon after awakening, which is when blood or saliva levels are usually obtained (Keevil et al., 2014).

Measuring *prenatal* levels of testosterone is especially difficult. The most precise way involves sampling the amniotic fluid surrounding the developing fetus (Sarkar et al., 2008). A few studies have derived samples from the placenta soon after delivery with the assumption that this provides a rough gage of fetal exposure a few days prior to birth (Galiano et al., 2021). In recent years, a relatively crude method has been established involving the so-called *2D:4D finger length ratio*. Basically, the longer an individual's pointing finger compared to his/her ring finger provides a rough estimate of relatively low prenatal testosterone exposure (Eler, 2018; Mikac et al., 2016). Finally, some studies have *inferred* exposure to testosterone among twins based on the sex of their co-twin, often known as the *twin testosterone transfer hypothesis* (Tapp et al., 2011). If both siblings are boys, both should have testosterone levels in the male-typical range, and, if both siblings are girls, their testosterone levels should be in the female-typical range. However, when twins are of the opposite sex, boys are thought to have slightly lower male-typical exposure to testosterone than singleton males, while girls usually have exposure that is in the high female-typical range compared to singleton females (Miller, 1994; Talia et al., 2020). Examples of these methods for inferring brain exposure to testosterone will be cited as I subject ENA theory to empirical scrutiny.

2.3 Social Role Theory and ENA Theory Flowcharts

Before offering an assessment of how well social role theory and ENA theory can explain each one of the fifteen nearly certain USDs, I will present separate flowcharts for both theories. These two charts identify both theory's primary (overarching) variables and show how these variables predict USDs in cognition and behavior.

2.3.1 Social Role Theory

In the case of social role theory, Figure 2 shows that sociocultural factors interact with three basic physiological sex differences (i.e., males being taller and stronger and females being the only sex capable of bearing offspring). Together, these three factors are thought to be responsible for USDs is cognition and behavior. All other cognitive and behavioral sex differences are assumed to be unique and varied from one culture to another.

According to social role theory, societal sex roles regulate hormones, thereby providing the context in which individual thinking and behavior are impacted (Eagly & Wood, 2012, p. 465; Wood & Eagly, 2012, p. 58). One can see in Figure 2 that social role theory includes "hormonal regulations" as contributing

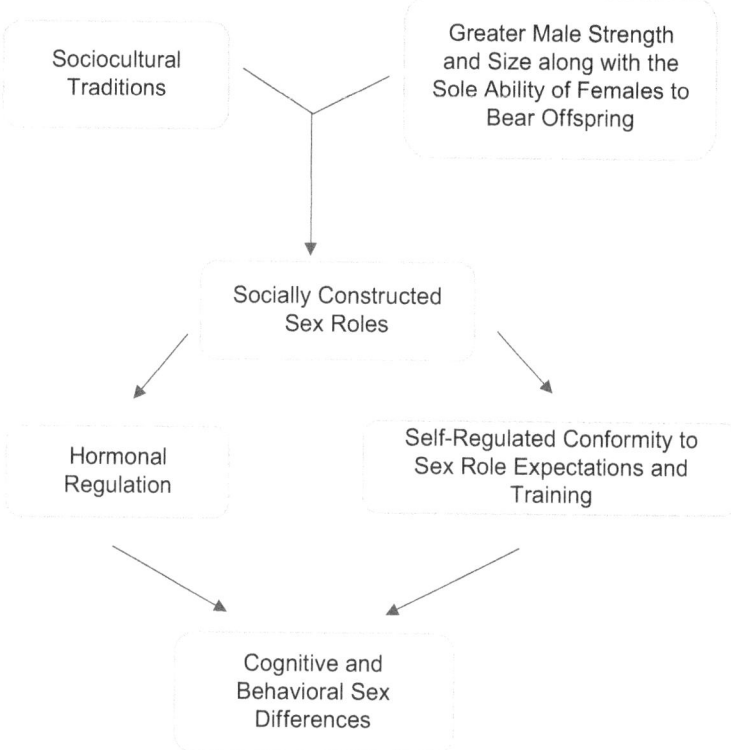

Figure 2 A flowchart summary of the social role theory of sex differences in cognition and behavior. Adapted from Eagly & Wood, 2012, p. 465 and Wood & Eagly, 2012, p. 58.

to cognitive and behavioral sex differences. However, this concept is vague and fails to provide any specifics regarding how "hormonal regulations" impact cognitive and behavioral sex differences.

2.3.2 ENA Theory

The flowchart for ENA theory is presented in Figure 3. It identifies two separate causal categories: one focusing on "why" USDs exist (the evolutionary factors) and the other pertaining to "how" these sex differences are physiologically regulated (the neurochemical factors). In evolutionary terms, sexual selection is seen as driving males and females apart in various ways so that each sex can pass genes on to future generations. Especially in mammals, where females must gestate each offspring (and usually breastfeed each one for substantial time thereafter), they are shown as having been sexually selected for biasing their mate choices in favor of males who appear capable of sustained resource provisioning. Furthermore, this female bias is hypothesized to have favored

EVOLUTIONARY FACTORS

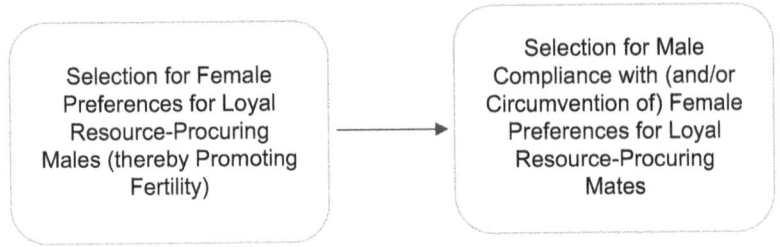

NEUROHOMONAL FACTORS

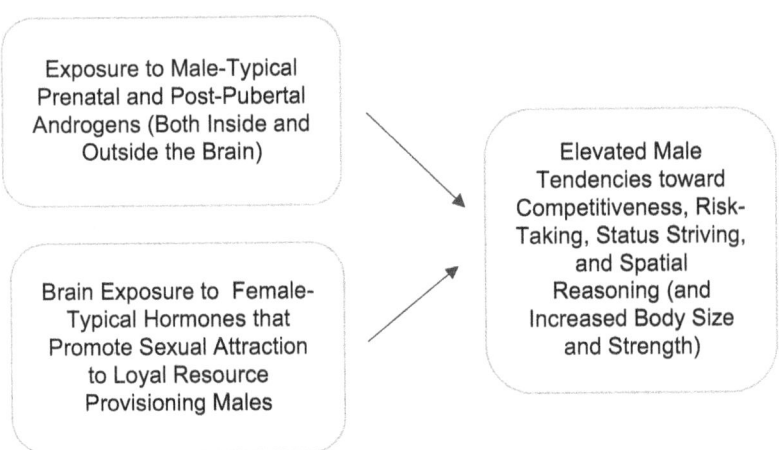

Figure 3 A flowchart summary of the ENA theory of sex differences in cognition and behavior. Adapted from Ellis, 2011.

males with resource provisioning tendencies. In other words, resource provisioning males will have a reproductive advantage over males who do otherwise. Also, once pregnant and breastfeeding, women who provision on their own will usually pass on fewer genes to future generations than women who can rely on resources provided by a mate.

The neurohormonal component of ENA theory is represented in the bottom segment of Figure 3. It asserts that genes (especially ones on the Y chromosome) interact to impact male cognition and behavior to help males conform to female mate preferences. Many of these genes regulate the production of sex hormones, especially testosterone.

In the case of females, genes promoting preferences for males with resource provisioning skills will have been favored by sexual selection. Among males, genes that promote abilities and interests to comply with female preferences will be sexually selected. At the present time, ENA theory can still be improved if the precise hormonal regimens involved in these evolved cognitive and behavioral traits can be more precisely identified. Nonetheless, several lines of evidence point toward combinations of testosterone and estrogens (and possibly progesterone levels), all being involved (e.g., De Jonge et al., 1986; Van Goozen et al., 1997).

One can see in both flowcharts that both theories hypothesize the involvement of hormonal factors in bringing about sex differences in cognition and behavior. However, ENA theory is more specific in this regard in four respects: First, it names the primary hormone (i.e., testosterone). Second, it specifies the direction of the main influence (i.e., greater testosterone produces more male-typical cognition and behavioral traits). Third, it identifies that the timing of testosterone's influences on cognition and behavior occurs both prenatally and postpubertally. Fourth, ENA theory stipulates that, to impact cognition and behavior, testosterone primarily operates on the brain.

Figure 2 shows that social role theory is nonspecific about hormonal contributions to sex differences in cognition and behavior, the timing of these contributions, or the involvement of the brain in the process. These features of social role theory make it all but impossible to scientifically test regarding any hormonal contributions to sex differences in cognition and behavior. Philosophers of science have long recognized that the best scientific theories are those that make the most predictions of what will eventually be empirically confirmed (Maxwell, 1974; Popper, 2013).

Throughout the remainder of this Element, I will assume that all fifteen variables identified in Table 1 are USDs, although the basic information supporting this assumption is provided in the table (which in turn summarizes the pertinent studies provided in our book). Overall, the primary goal will now be to determine which of the two theories can best account for *why* these fifteen variables would be culturally universal. The narrative assessment will consider each of the fifteen variables one at a time.

3 Applying Social Role Theory and ENA Theory to Each One of the 15 Nearly Certain Universal Sex Differences in Cognition and Behavior

As already explained, the last two columns of Table 1 provide four symbols that are used to summarize how well both theories can account for each of the fifteen

USDs. First, an *x* is used to indicate that a theory is essentially silent regarding a particular sex difference. Second, if a theory can provide a plausible *argument* to explain a USD, although no independent support for this argument was found, a single checkmark (✓) is provided. Third, if there are both reasonable theoretical arguments for a particular sex difference being universal, and *some* independent empirical support was located in support of the argument, double checkmarks (✓✓) are assigned to the theory. Finally, three checkmarks (✓✓✓) are used to denote that not only are plausible theoretical arguments apparent but also *substantial* independent empirical support was located. If readers can provide me with any additional relevant empirical evidence, I will acknowledge the oversight in an erratum.

3.1 Variable 1: Earnings, USD-Male

The first variable listed in Table 1 constitutes the most extensively investigated USD that our book was able to identify. It involves sex differences in earnings. As shown in Column 3, a total of 579 studies were found, 571 of which concluded that the average salaries (or other income measures) for males surpassed those of females. Column 5 of Table 1 shows that forty-seven different countries were sampled along with an additional fifty-eight studies derived from two or more countries.

Regarding the eight exceptions, none of them posed significant threats to the generalization that male salaries surpass those of females. Six of the exceptional studies were based on clearly nonrepresentative samples. For instance, two studies were limited to blacks living in Britain, one involved a sample of intellectually disabled persons, and the remaining three studies had to do with newly hired college graduates. The final two exceptional studies were experimental in nature. Both involved asking prospective employers to report what salaries they would offer hypothetical men and women with identical job credentials for a specific type of job and reported no significant differences.

Overall, our book's review of studies pertaining to sex differences in earnings provides essentially irrefutable evidence that, in all societies, male workers earn more than female workers. In other words, earned salaries is a USD-Male. Attention now turns to how well each of the two theories can account for this USD.

3.1.1 Social Role Theory

To explain USDs in average salaries or other types of income, social role theory can draw on the fact that only females can become pregnant. Thus, at least for women who bear children, they are likely to periodically interrupt their involvement in the paid workforce to devote time to providing childcare, especially if they routinely breastfeed after giving birth. Substantial evidence supports this line of reasoning (Cebrián & Moreno, 2015; de Quinto et al., 2021), especially for women who begin having child early in life (Putz & Engelhardt-Woelfler, 2014) and for those living in countries with few paid work-leave accommodations (Karimi, 2014). Furthermore, one study indicated that most of the adverse impact of childbearing on female earnings occurred in the first few years after giving birth, and that the impact was no longer significant after fifteen years of a woman's last birth (Angelov & Karimi, 2012).

Also supporting the view that pregnancy among females is a major cause of sex disparities in wages, a Danish study indicated that, before women give birth, their salaries were statistically equal to those of males. However, after giving birth, the average salaries for males begin to surpass that of females (Kleven et al., 2019).

Obviously, these pregnancy-related work interruptions are bound to adversely affect career advancement, which is detrimental to salary increases. This "penalties of motherhood" explanation of sex differences in earnings has been criticized as providing only a weak explanation for sex differences in earnings, arguing instead for an explanation rooted in the types of occupations both sexes choose (England, 2005). Nonetheless, it is entirely consistent with sex role theory.

Another study involved persons who never married. It reported that men still earned more than women (Cutler & Harootyan, 1975). This study also indicated that the types of jobs males and females tend to choose seems to be far more important in explaining sex differences in wages than sex differences in the ability to bear offspring. Later, under the discussion of Variable 14, I will elaborate on the possible importance of sex difference in occupational choices. It has to do with being educated in the physical sciences and engineering.

Proponents of social role theory have also argued that, because males are taller and physically stronger than females, they are often able to achieve greater social dominance (Eagly & Wood, 2012), one result of which is often higher average earnings (Cheng & Tracy, 2014). One way to independently test this reasoning would involve documenting that, even *within* each sex, height and/or physical strength are positively correlated with average income. Studies have found a great deal of support for this latter hypothesis, especially regarding height (Judge & Cable, 2004; review: Ellis et al., 2018, p. 259).

Overall, social role theory offers explanations for why males in all known societies earn more on average than females. The theory does so by attributing the differences to the fact that pregnancy has suppressing effects on earnings and by noting that males exhibit greater height and strength than females, which promotes greater dominance. These explanations have substantial empirical support, thereby justifying three checkmarks in Table 1 for this theory.

3.1.2 ENA Theory

Both the evolutionary and the neurohormonal components of ENA theory can provide explanations for sex differences in average earnings. Some of its explanations parallel those offered by social role theory and others diverge.

Regarding evolution, ENA theory argues that females have been sexually selected for making mate choices based on indications that a prospective mate is competent at resource provisioning. Without this male ability, the females will usually have to curtail their production of offspring or at least provide less care to them (Ellis, 2001). Theoretically, this would be especially true in societies where little governmental support is given to mothers who are pregnant or with dependent children and nonsupportive fathers. Thus, whether their choices are made consciously or not, women who bias their mate selection in favor of males who appear to be willing and capable provisioners of resources will increase their chances of passing genes (and genes of their mates) on to subsequent generations.

This evolutionary argument can also be applied to males. Presumably, males have been sexually selected for their abilities to comply with female preferences regarding resource provisioning. In other words, males who become competent and reliable resource provisioners will usually pass their genes on to future generations at higher rates than other males. The main qualification to this generalization involves males who use deception or force to obtain copulatory access (Ellis & Hoskin, 2015).

Besides evidence that males on average earn more than females, there is additional evidence supporting this evolutionary reasoning. As will be discussed more regarding Variable 13, studies throughout the world have shown that females *prefer* mates who are, or appear to be, "good providers" to a greater degree than do males. This suggests that sexual selection for high-earning males is likely to still be ongoing.

Another line of evidence that is consistent with using the sexual selection argument for sex differences in earnings comes from research indicating that males consider monetary compensation for their work as being more important than do females (review: Ellis et al., 2024b, pp. 941–943). In other words, women appear to have greater interests in jobs where the work environment is clean and friendly (review: Ellis et al., 2024b, pp. 937–938), while men focus more on earnings, no matter what the job entails. Overall, the evolutionary component of ENA theory appears to have considerable evidentiary support.

Turning to the physiological aspects of ENA theory, brain exposure to testosterone should be positively correlated with how much individuals earn. Evidence in this regard has been somewhat mixed regarding prenatal testosterone. One study was based on a sample of twins. As already noted, studies have indicated that female fetuses who share the womb with male fetuses usually exhibit at least slightly masculinized behavioral traits when compared to singleton-born females. This is true for studies of both nonhumans (review: Ryan & Vandenbergh, 2002) as well as humans (Cohen-Bendahan et al., 2005; Miller, 1994). Such masculinizing tendencies appear to be the result of females with male co-twins being exposed to higher-than-normal amounts of prenatal testosterone than females who share the womb with other females.

Following this line of reasoning, ENA theory predicts that fetuses sharing the womb with an opposite-sex co-twin should have higher lifetime earnings than those with same-sex co-twins. In other words, when one co-twin is secreting male-typical levels of testosterone during gestation and one is only secreting female-typical levels, the latter is likely to receive above average exposure to testosterone. Some evidence has been reported on this theoretical line of reasoning. One study of earnings by adult twins indicated that male–male co-twins had higher average lifetime earnings than did male–female co-twins. In the case of females, however, the sex of the co-twin was not significantly correlated with lifetime earnings (Gielen et al., 2016). Another study of twins reported that females with a male co-twin earned *less* than did females with a female co-twin (Bütikofer et al., 2019). Overall, the results from these two studies provide little support for ENA theory.

Another study designed to estimate prenatal testosterone exposure used the 2D:4D finger length ratio. The study reported that a significant positive correlation existed between prenatal testosterone exposure (i.e., relatively low 2D:4D ratios) and wages in adulthood among women but not among males (Nye, Yudkevich et al., 2014). This finding is obviously mixed regarding providing support of ENA theory.

Two other studies of prenatal testosterone exposure looked for evidence that high exposure promotes desires to be self-employed (rather than working for others). Such research is relevant here to the extent that self-employed persons have relatively higher incomes (including profits) than do persons who work for others (Bernhardt, 1994; Schneck, 2020). One study of self-employment among men found it to be positively correlated with prenatal testosterone exposure, as indicated by low 2D:4D ratios (Hughes & Kumari, 2019). The other study also reported that, among both sexes, persons who were self-employed had 2D:4D ratios indicative of higher prenatal testosterone exposure (Nicolaou et al., 2018).

In addition to prenatal testosterone, ENA theory also predicts that postpubertal testosterone (often called *circulating testosterone*) should contribute to earnings. Four relevant studies were located. These studies were based on samples of men, and all of them indicated that significant positive correlations were evident (Coates & Herbert, 2008; Harrison et al., 2021; Hughes & Kumari, 2019; Luoto et al., 2021). In other words, on average, men with relatively high circulating testosterone levels appear to earn more than men with low circulating levels.

Overall, findings have been somewhat mixed regarding the effects of brain exposure to testosterone on lifetime earnings regarding prenatal testosterone exposure. However, in the case of circulating testosterone levels among adults, the predicted positive correlation has been strongly supported.

How can the apparent positive relationship between testosterone and earnings be explained? Much of the answer seems to involve noting that exposing the brain to high testosterone has been shown to promote competitiveness (Apicella et al., 2011; Simmons & Roney, 2011; Eisenegger et al., 2017) as well as risk-taking (Mehta et al., 2008; Volman et al., 2011; Welker et al., 2015). Both personality traits, in turn, have been found to be positively associated with earnings (Hughes & Kumari, 2019). More will be said about testosterone and risk-taking when Variable 12 is discussed. Because both the evolutionary component and the postpubertal aspects of the physiological component of ENA theory are strongly supported, it receives three checkmarks for explaining sex differences in average earnings.

3.2 Variable 2: Performing Household Chores, USD-Female

As shown in Table 1, the second-best documented USD involves performing indoor household chores such as laundry, cooking, and cleaning. A total of 334 studies were found bearing on this sex difference, 331 of which concluded that females surpass males. The number of countries sampled was thirty-one along with forty-one multinational studies.

There were three exceptions, all of which were limited to samples of children. For the 301 studies involving adolescents and/or adults, there were no exceptions. Thus, on average, from adolescence onward, our literature review indicated that females throughout the world surpass males in the amount of time spent performing indoor household chores.

3.2.1 Social Role Theory

For many years, proponents of social role theory have argued that sex differences in doing housework reflect cultural traditions (Hoffman, 1977; Lachance-Grzela & Bouchard, 2010; Lennon, 1994) and sex role stereotypes (Eagly et al., 2000). Both explanations lead one to expect that there should be some cultures in which the sexes are equal, or where males actually do more household chores than females. Table 1 shows that, at least among adolescents and adults, this is not the case.

Social role theory assumes that while all behavioral sex differences are culturally learned, biological sex differences (such as physical strength and bearing offspring) can sometimes produce USDs in behavior. Could doing housework be one such example? Perhaps. Based on social role theory, one could argue that because only females can bear offspring and breastfeed them, they are likely to end up spending more time in the home (Wood & Eagly, 2012, p. 59). Thus, because of sex differences associated with childbirth and rearing, females are likely to be more inclined to maintain a clean and orderly indoor environment and would have more opportunities to do so.

While this line of reasoning cannot be considered disproven, it is challenged by other evidence. Specifically, even for individuals living along (Kanazawa, 2005, p. 283) and cohabitate with no children (Batalova & Cohen, 2002), females still perform more housework than do males. Furthermore, one study of dual-earning couples without children also concluded that women spend more time doing housework than men (Evertsson, 2014).

Overall, there is no reason to doubt that women perform more household cleaning and maintenance chores than do men throughout the world. From the perspective of social role theory, this universal sex difference can be attributed to long cultural traditions possibly rooted in the fact that, because only females bear children, they feel obliged to fulfill homemaking duties. However, because no specific empirical evidence was found to support this line of reasoning, I assigned social role theory an "x" regarding the universality of this variable.

3.2.2 ENA Theory

Both the evolutionary and neurohormonal components of ENA theory can be seen as addressing the issue of sex differences in performing household chores. Regarding evolution, scientists have noted that, especially among mammals, females can identify their offspring with greater certainty than can males (Buss & Schmitt, 1993; Dixson, 2009). As a result, females will have been more strongly favored for providing care to offspring. At least among humans, one expression of caring for offspring would focus on health, among the expressions of which would entail maintaining a clean and hazard-free home environment (Preston, 2013).

In accordance with this line of reasoning, while differences are modest, research indicates that females have a keener sense of smell than do males (review: Ellis et al., 2024b, pp. 12–13; Sorokowski et al. 2019). Also, some research indicated that genetic factors may be partly responsible for sex differences in the ability to detect odors (Hoover, 2010; Majid et al., 2017).

Moreover, a potentially relevant line of evidence comes from outside the human species. It involves a phenomenon known as "nest sanitation behavior" among birds (Blair & Tucker, 1941; Skutch, 1976, p. 282). In about 20 percent of bird species, breeding pairs of males and females co-parent their chicks (Heinsohn & Double, 2004). Besides both parents cooperatively feeding their nestlings, they also rid the nest of debris such as parasites, broken eggshells, and especially fecal sacs produced by the chicks. Researchers have reported that while there may be exceptions, in most co-parenting bird species, females devote more time to keeping their nests clean than do their male partners (review: Guigueno & Sealy, 2012).

Returning to humans, our book identified fourteen studies having to do with sex differences in people's tendencies to be health conscious. Every one of these fourteen studies concluded that females were more so than males (review: Ellis et al., 2024b, pp. 837–838). Similarly, the vast majority of fifty-one studies of sex differences in the taking of preventive health measures concluded that females surpass males in this regard (review: Ellis et al., 2024c, pp. 92–93). Thus, considerable independent research points toward females being more concerned with cleanliness and health than are males.

Regarding evolution, it is reasonable to suspect that females may have been more strongly favored than males for being health conscious, not only for themselves but also for their offspring. If so, one expression of health consciousness could be a greater desire for household cleanliness among females, ergo greater tendencies to perform household chores.

If evolutionary forces have helped to produced sex differences in traits such as doing more housework, ENA theory hypothesizes that neurohormonal processes should also be involved. Specifically, brain exposure to testosterone should *inhibit* spending time performing household chores. This is obviously a testable hypothesis, but I found no relevant evidence. Because of the empirical evidence supporting the evolutionary arm of ENA theory but no evidence bearing on the physiological arm, I just assigned two checkmarks to this variable in Table 1.

3.3 Variable 3: Self-Reported Criminality, USD-Male

Criminal behavior comes in many forms and can be assessed in different ways, although the most common types of measures involve either official data (e.g., arrests and convictions) or self-reports (usually on anonymous questionnaires). Regarding the latter, 233 studies of self-reported criminality (including delinquency) were located. All but six of these studies concluded that males self-reported significantly more involvement than females. Of the six exceptions, five pertained to minor forms of delinquency (e.g., truancy, running away from home, under-age drinking, and marijuana use). The one study of adults that found no significant sex difference was based on a sample of prisoners, obviously not representative of a general population. A total of forty-six different countries were sampled in addition to seven multinational studies.

The findings regarding self-reported criminality strongly indicates that males are more likely to engage in criminal and delinquent conduct than females, especially regarding serious types of offenses such as major thefts and assaults. How well do the two theories explain this universal sex difference? In making my assessments, I will assume that males and females are equally honest in reporting their offending histories.

3.3.1 Social Role Theory

Social role theory is likely to explain sex differences in criminal and delinquent behavior by noting that males have greater physical strength. Physical strength could give males more confidence in winning when engaging in physical aggression (Eagly & Wood, 2012, p. 465). Of course, this would have no bearing on most property and drug offenses, which also appears to be more prevalent among males than among females (review: Ellis et al., 2019, pp. 55–56).

Overall, no independent empirical evidence could be found to support social role theory's explanation for why most forms of self-reported criminality appears to be more prevalent among males than among females. However, one could argue that throughout the world, antisocial behavior is more likely to be tolerated and/or expected among males than among females (due to men's greater physical strength). For this reason, and because sex differences in violent forms of crime can be predicted with social role theory (as I will discuss regarding Variable 15 further), I have assigned social role theory one checkmark beside Variable 3 in Table 1.

3.3.2 ENA Theory

ENA theory's explanation for sex differences in self-reported criminality comes from both of its evolutionary and physiological components (Ellis & Hoskin, 2015). Regarding evolution, the theory makes three assumptions regarding sex differences in criminality (Ellis, 2001). First, females have been sexually selected for preferring mates with the ability to provide resources. Second, males with the greatest likelihood of passing genes onto future generations will have relatively strong tendencies to comply with this female preference (Fales et al., 2016; Waynforth, 2001; Wiederman, 1993), and this compliance would have little to do with whether legal or illegal means are used to obtain the resources. Third, males can sometimes pass their genes on to future generations by using force or deception to obtain mates, thereby circumventing the tendencies females may have evolved to choose mates with resources. This latter assumption takes ENA theory into the realm of sexual assault, the commission of which has been shown to be much more common among males than females, although the number of studies fell short of 100 (Ellis et al., 2024c, pp. 526–528).

Turning to the physiological aspects of ENA theory, substantial evidence points toward brain exposure to testosterone as promoting several victimizing forms of criminal behavior. In this regard, numerous studies have indicated that *both* prenatal and postpubertal testosterone levels are positively correlated with criminality, especially among males (Ellis et al., 2019, pp. 353–358). Overall, the neurohormonal aspects of ENA theory appears to have substantial empirical support regarding sex differences in self-reported criminality. For this reason, I assigned it three checkmarks.

3.4 Variable 4: Official Criminality, USD-Male

The fourth variable listed in Table 1 involves the commission of crime based on official criminal justice statistics (such as arrest and conviction data). As one would suspect, official data usually pertain to much more serious forms of criminality than is the case for the average self-reported offense (Babinski et al., 2001).

One can see in Table 1 that all but 2 of the 191 pertinent studies concluded that official criminality is more prevalent among males than among females. Both exceptions involved being detained for adolescent delinquency (for which there were no significant sex differences). In the case of adult criminality, there were no exceptions. The number of countries sampled in these studies was thirty, along with ten additional studies that were multinational in coverage.

3.4.1 Social Role Theory

As noted regarding self-reported offending (Variable 3), social role theory has difficulty explaining why males are universally involved in official criminality than females. One reason for this difficulty involves noting that social role theorists consider the criminal justice system as a male-dominated institution used to control women and other subjugated people (Covington & Bloom, 2003; Eagly, 1987). If so, it is difficult to explain why most of those subjected to arrest, prosecution, and punishment would be males.

Perhaps, one could account for why official criminal behavior is more common among males using social role theory by assuming that the commission of crimes is enhanced by men's greater size and strength. There is some support for this idea. Specifically, among males, criminals do appear to be more muscular than males in general, especially for violent offending (review: Ellis et al., 2019, pp. 341–342). Regarding height, however, findings have been inconsistent regarding any specific within-sex association with criminality (review: Ellis et al., 2019, pp. 339–341). Overall, the absence of independent empirical evidence warrants assigning social role theory two checkmarks for Variable 4.

3.4.2 ENA Theory

To explain why males are more likely than females to be involved in the commission of officially measured crime throughout the world, ENA theory can draw on both evolutionary and neurohormonal variables. In evolutionary terms, most victimizing forms of criminality can be seen as being (a) efforts to obtain resources (that males can often use to attract mates), (b) forms of competition with other males for mating opportunities with females, and/or (c) sexual assaults on females directly (Daly, 2017; Ellis & Hoskin, 2015). This means that criminality can sometimes help males contribute genes to subsequent generations just as do noncriminal forms of competition for resources and/or mating opportunities.

Regarding neurohormonal factors, considerable evidence indicates that victimizing forms of criminality are positively correlated with both prenatal and postpubertal testosterone levels (review: Ellis et al., 2019, pp. 351–355). It is also worth mentioning that risk-taking has been found to be positively correlated with involvement in crime and delinquency (Wilson & Daly, 1985; review: Ellis et al., 2019, pp. 219–221). This comports with evidence that risk-taking is more prevalent among males than females (see Variable 12 for evidence in this regard). Finally, risk-taking appears to be promoted by exposing the brain to testosterone (review: Apicella et al., 2015; Ronay & Von Hippel, 2010; also see Variable 12). Given the weight of evidence that both prenatal and postpubertal testosterone is related to criminality, I have entered three checkmarks for ENA theory's explanation of sex differences beside this variable in Table 1.

3.5 Variable 5: Engaging in Physical Exercise, USD-Male

The fifth USD variable listed in Table 1 pertains to physical exercise. One can see that a total of 149 studies were located, 142 of which concluded that males engage in more physical exercise than do females. All seven exceptional studies simply reported no significant sex differences and were found to have focused on *moderate* degrees of exercise. All studies of *vigorous* exercise concluded that males surpass females. A total of eighteen different countries were sampled, along with four studies of two or more countries.

3.5.1 Social Role Theory

If one assumes that physical strength is associated with involvement in greater physical exercise, social role theory can provide an explanation for why males engage in more physical exercise than females. Supporting this theoretical reasoning, research has found physical strength and physical exercise are positively correlated (Haynes & DeBeliso, 2019). Furthermore, at least some of the positive association between exercise and strength appears to be due to the fact that exercise promotes physical strength (Buriticá-Marínet al., 2023; Rismayanthi et al., 2022). Unfortunately, social role theory provides no guidance for assessing *why* sex differences in strength would actually promote sex differences in physical exercise. Therefore, I have provided a single checkmark to this theory's explanation of sex differences in vigorous exercise.

3.5.2 ENA Theory

The ENA theory offers both an evolutionary and a physiological explanation for why sex differences in physical exercise is found throughout the world. In evolutionary terms, physical exercise is likely to have been favored among males more than females, especially in pre-industrial societies, as a way of enhancing their abilities to obtain resources with which to attract mates and help them rear offspring. More specifically, engaging in frequent exercise would promote men's success at hunting and tending livestock, as well as engaging in strenuous manual laborers (Pettay et al., 2007; Smith, 2004).

Regarding the physiological aspects of the theory, research has shown that when muscles are exposed to testosterone, physical strength is enhanced (Auyeung et al., 2011; Storer et al., 2008). Furthermore, when the brain is exposed to testosterone, physical activity tends to rise (Lightfoot, 2008; Vaamonde et al. 2012). These findings suggest that when both muscle tissue and nervous tissue are exposed to testosterone, the effects are synergistic. Furthermore, not only does testosterone help to promote physical exertion but physical exertion in turn also promotes testosterone production (Kumagai et al. 2018; Riachy et al. 2020).

Experiments with laboratory animals have indicated that part of the enhanced physical activity that testosterone promotes is mediated by the release of the neurotransmitter, dopamine (Jardí et al., 2018). Overall, physical exercise, especially when strenuous, is more common among males than among females, and ENA theory provides empirically supported arguments for explaining these relationships, earning it three checkmarks in Table 1.

3.6 Variable 6: Occupational Prominence, USD-Male

Only a minority of individuals in any profession or business will attain prominence no matter how *prominence* is operationalized. Using a variety of different measures, many studies have assessed sex differences in tendencies to become prominent in one's occupationally pursuits. As shown in Table 1, out of 148 studies, 146 have concluded that males are more likely to attain prominence in their line of work than are females. The two exceptional findings simply found no statistically significant difference. Twenty-two individual countries were sampled in these studies along with twenty additional studies of multiple countries.

Before considering how well the two theories can account for this apparent universal sex difference, it is worth mentioning that part of the explanation for sex differences in occupational prominence involves the fact that males spend more time working outside the home than do females (review: Ellis et al., 2024c, pp. 647–650). Also, males are more likely to be involved in entrepreneurial and supervisory occupations (review: Ellis et al., 2024c, pp. 665 & 662), jobs involving elected offices (review: Ellis et al., 2024c, pp. 698–700), and the physical sciences and engineering (Ellis et al., 2014c, pp. 685–686, 696). Workers in these types of occupations often garner more recognition than workers in more mundane occupations.

3.6.1 Social Role Theory

The explanation offered by social role theory for sex differences in occupational prominence would involve noting that, because males bear no children, they can devote more time to developing and refining their occupational skills. One way to test this line of reasoning would involve comparing occupational prominence for men and women who have never had children. If social role theory is correct, occupational prominence among childless couples should not exhibit significant sex differences. In making such comparisons, it might also be necessary to exclude individuals who attain prominence in sports where physical strength could give males an edge.

Unfortunately, I found no studies pertaining to sex differences in occupational prominence among childless couples. Therefore, I assigned one checkmark to this theory in Table 1.

3.6.2 ENA Theory

To explain sex differences in occupational prominence from the perspective of ENA theory, one can draw on both its evolutionary and its neurohormonal components. In evolutionary terms, ENA theory would focus on female tendencies to prefer mates with resources along with recognizing that occupational prominence is often associated with the procurement of resources (Bereczkei et al. 1997; Ellis 2001; Souza et al., 2016). In other words, while not all prestigious occupations are associated with high incomes, very few fail to garner at least moderate monetary rewards (Garcia-Mainar et al., 2018; Magnusson, 2009).

Regarding the neurohormonal aspects of ENA theory, it predicts that relatively high brain exposure to testosterone should be associated with occupational prestige. Support for this hypothesis comes from studies indicating that status-striving behavior is positively correlated with both prenatal testosterone (Bijleveld & Baalbergen, 2017; Millet & Dewitte, 2008) and postpubertal circulating testosterone (Dabbs et al., 1990; Mazur & Booth, 1998). Exposure to prenatal testosterone among males also appears to be positively correlated with general competitiveness (Bönte et al., 2017).

While more research is needed, both the evolutionary and the physiological arms of ENA theory have substantial supportive independent evidence regarding sex differences in occupational prominence. For this reason, I gave ENA theory three checkmarks in Table 1.

3.7 Variable 7: Accidental Injuries, USD-Male

Sex differences in sustaining accidental injuries (including fatalities) have been widely studied. As shown in Table 1, all but 4 of the 134 pertinent studies concluded that males were significantly more likely than females to be physically injured. The four exceptions had to do with accidental injuries attributable to falls, which appear to be more common among postmenopausal women than men of comparable age. Studies located were conducted in seventeen different countries along with eleven multinational studies.

As to why adult females may sometimes suffer more accidental injuries due to falls than adult males, it is likely the result of thinner bone density, especially following menopause (Jarvinen & Kannus, 1997; Tosi et al., 2005). I will set this issue aside when interpreting the two theories for explaining why nearly all studies have concluded that males sustain nearly all types of accidental injuries more than females.

3.7.1 Social Role Theory

Using social role theory to explain why males suffer more accidental injuries than females (except possibly for persons over the age of fifty) is difficult. About the only way to do so would involve asserting that physical strength promotes physical activity, which in turn increases the likelihood of accidental injuries. However, as noted earlier (under Variable 5), social role theory provides no way of logically connecting physical strength with physical activity. Granting that social role theory might hypothesize that physical strength promotes physical activity and therefore greater risk of being injured, I have given this theory a single checkmark for explaining sex differences in sustaining accidental injuries.

3.7.2 ENA Theory

Later in the section, Variable 12 will document that males take more risks (or express a greater willingness to do so) than do females. At the present junction, this sex differences can be invoked to help account for sex differences in accidental injuries. From an evolutionary perspective, scientists have argued that risk-taking is more likely to benefit males than females. This is partly due to the contribution that risk-taking can make toward the procurement and retention of resources (Baker & Maner, 2008; Maxfield et al., 2010). Of course, an unfortunate side effect of risk-taking, at least in physical terms, is an elevated probability of accidental injuries (Turner et al., 2004).

Turning to the physiological aspect of ENA theory, no research was found directly linking testosterone to accidental injuries. However, as will be documented under Variable 12, substantial evidence points toward a positive correlation between testosterone and risk-taking (Apicella et al., 2015; Dariotis et al., 2016; Votinov et al. 2022; reviews: Kurath & Mata, 2018). Therefore, ENA theory has considerable support when it comes to explaining why males suffer more accidental injuries than females, leading to its being assigned three checkmarks in Table 1.

3.8 Variable 8: Elected Office Holder, USD-Male

Many studies have assessed sex differences among elected political office holders. As one can see in Table 1, 127 out of 129 studies indicated that males are more likely to hold these positions than females. The two exceptions simply reported no significant differences. Twenty-two different countries were sampled along with twenty-two multinational studies.

3.8.1 Social Role Theory

The only way social role theory appears capable of explaining why males would be more likely than females to hold elective political offices would involve the fact that only females can become pregnant. In this regard, it is reasonable to assume that pregnancy curtails the ability of women to spend time campaigning for elective offices. One way to test this hypothesis would be to determine if women with no children are statistically equivalent to men in their tendencies to hold elected office. No such research was located, so I assigned social role theory a single checkmark regarding its potential for explaining sex differences in tendencies to hold elected political office.

3.8.2 ENA Theory

The ENA theory offers both an evolutionary and physiological accounts for sex differences in elected office holding. Regarding evolution, in many species, females are more likely than males to mate with individuals who display dominant behavior than to those who do not (Weisfeld & Dillon, 2012, p. 25). This apparent attraction to dominant males probably has to do with the fact that dominance is generally associated with control over territory and the resources it contains (Anderson et al., 2012; Smuts, 1995). If holding political office at least roughly depends on displaying dominance and resource control, it is likely to attract mates, even among humans. More will be discussed in this regard under Variable 13, having to do with mate preferences.

In terms of a physiological explanation, several studies have found evidence that brain exposure to testosterone promotes tendencies to pursue power and to achieve dominance and social status. Regarding prenatal testosterone exposure, two 2D:4D finger length studies indicated that high exposure was associated with status-striving later in life (Neave et al., 2003; Moffit & Swanik, 2011).

Regarding postpubertal (circulating) testosterone levels, at least five studies of males have found significant positive correlations between testosterone and status-striving behavior (Arnocky et al., 2018; Dabbs & Dabbs, 2000; Määttänen et al., 2013; Mazur & Booth 1998; Tremblay, 1998). Two studies of females came to the same conclusion (Cashdan, 1995; Grant & France, 2001). Similar associations have been reported for dominance-striving behavior among nonhuman animals (Helle et al., 2008; Perret, 2018). Overall, if one assumes that serving in an elective office partially reflects a form of status-striving, ENA theory provides an explanation for why males in all societies are more likely to hold elected offices than females. Therefore, I assigned three checkmarks to this variable for ENA theory in Table 1.

3.9 Variable 9: ADHD, USD-Male

Attention deficit hyperactivity disorder (ADHD) refers to tendencies to fidget frequently, to avoid paying attention to teachers and parents, and to often being disruptive when in group settings (Asherson, 2005). The condition is most often diagnosed among school-aged children and young adolescents. Based on samples drawn from eighteen countries, all but 2 of the 126 studies concluded that males surpass females in being diagnosed with ADHD. The two exceptions simply found no significant sex difference.

3.9.1 Social Role Theory

Nothing in social role theory seems to provide any way to account for why ADHD would be more common among males than females throughout the world. Therefore, it is listed in Table 1 as being silent regarding this sex difference.

3.9.2 ENA Theory

As already noted regarding Variable 5, males appear to have been evolutionarily favored for being more physically active than females (Cordain et al., 1998; Jonason, 2007; Wilson et al., 2009). In foraging societies, high activity levels could promote exploratory and predatory behavior. For humans living in more technologically advanced societies, high activity levels could increase the chances of obtaining resources with which to attract mates.

While evolutionary reasoning can provide a possible explanation for why males would surpass females in *average* activity levels, one is still left wondering why a minority of males would be unusually hyperactive and inattentive. The answer may lie in noting that most evolved traits take on roughly normal curves of distribution, with population means being what is *most* favored (Parker, 1974; Stearns, 1993). Accordingly, one can imagine two overlapping normal curves, one for males and one for females, regarding tendencies to be hyperactive. Because of sexual selection for traits linked to high activity levels, more males would be at the extreme right end of this normal curve. Thus, greater proportions of males than females would be diagnosed as exhibiting ADHD.

In line with this evolutionary reasoning, findings from three recent studies are worth noting. Two of these studies found that children who exhibit at least modest degrees of ADHD were *more* likely than boys in general to eventually become successful business owners (Lerner et al., 2019; Moore et al., 2021). If we assume that business ownership is more likely to result in above average incomes compared working for wages (see Bernhardt, 1994; Schneck, 2020), a positive relationship between entrepreneurship and at least modest forms of ADHD is predictable.

The third study was based on a computer-simulated foraging experiment. It indicated that persons with ADHD ranged further afield than did persons in general. This finding was interpreted as suggesting that ADHD traits may have evolved to promote the use of relatively risky resource-securing strategies (Barack et al., 2022).

Turning to the possibility that brain exposure to testosterone contributes to sex differences in ADHD, there is a great deal of evidentiary support. In the case of prenatal testosterone, seven studies have reported significant within-sex relationships between 2D:4D and ADHD symptoms (Akkuş & Avşar, 2024;

De Bruin et al., 2006; Martel et al., 2008; McFadden et al., 2005; Roberts & Martel, 2013; Stevenson, et al., 2007; Wang et al., 2017), although one study reported no significant relationship (Lemiere et al., 2010).

Regarding postpubertal testosterone, the evidence has been mixed (review: Camara et al., 2022). Such findings are not particularly surprising, however, given that ADHD symptoms are primarily diagnosed prior to the onset of puberty. To summarize, ENA theory seems to provide reasonable explanations for why ADHD is more common among males than among females in all countries ever studied. Nevertheless, because of a few inconsistencies in the current evidence, I have assigned two checkmarks to ENA theory for explaining this sex difference.

3.10 Variable 10: Conduct Disorder, USD-Male

While childhood misbehavior can be defined in many ways and varies a great deal in degrees, few parents, guardians, or teachers would dispute that some children are rather extreme in this regard. The term *conduct disorder* (also known as *childhood conduct disorder*) refers to unusually high tendencies for children to be socially destructive, deceitful, and aggressive. These children also tend to be unusually defiant toward parents, teachers, or others who try to restrain their frequent misconduct (Fairchild et al., 2019).

Table 1 shows that nearly all studies have concluded that males are more likely than females to be diagnosed with conduct disorder, especially when aggression is a significant part of the diagnosis. Specifically, 126 out of 132 studies came to this conclusion. All six of the exceptions simply reported no significant sex differences. Samples for these studies were obtained from nineteen different countries in addition to one multicountry study.

3.10.1 Social Role Theory

The only way social role theory seems capable of explaining why conduct disorder is more common among males than females would entail attributing the difference to the fact that males are taller and physically stronger than females. In other words, given that conduct disorder is often associated with physical aggression, persons who are larger and stronger might stereotype themselves (and be stereotyped by others) as being more likely to get away with being physically aggressive in order to achieve their goals. Such an explanation, however, would be weakened by the fact that conduct disorder is usually diagnosed in childhood, years before sex differences in height and physical strength are detectable (Ellis et al., 2024a, pp. 48, 145–147). For this reason, I have given an *x* (meaning *no explanation*) to social role theory's ability to explain sex differences in conduct disorder.

3.10.2 ENA Theory

From an evolutionary standpoint, ENA theory would anchor its explanation for sex differences in conduct disorder in the assumption that males have been reproductively favored for being relatively competitive, aggressive, and prone to take risks and that the underlying neurology is likely due to prenatal exposure to testosterone. Later in life, such sex differences would likely enhance an individual's tendencies to acquire resources with which to attract mates (Griskevicius et al., 2009; Wong & Candolin, 2005). Furthermore, it is worth reiterating the point that evolved traits will often vary around means that have been optimally favored.

As explained earlier regarding ADHD, at a population level, most evolved traits take on roughly normal (bell-shaped) distributions around their optimal reproductive value. This means that some individuals will exhibit these traits in ways that substantially undershoot *and* overshoot what is being naturally (including sexually) selected (Vercken et al., 2012). If we assume that the optimal expressions of traits – such as competitiveness, risk-taking, and aggression – is higher for males than for females, we should expect higher proportions of males than females to overshoot what is optimally favored as well. Such reasoning leads one to expect greater proportions of males to exhibit conduct disorders than females.

Regarding the possibility of brain exposure to testosterone promoting conduct disorder, some supportive evidence has appeared in the scientific literature. Specifically, two studies of adolescent males found significant positive correlations between circulating levels of testosterone and conduct disorder (Rowe et al., 2004; Kirillova et al., 2008).

In the case of prenatal testosterone, one study indicated that levels were positively correlated with "disruptive behavior" among males, although it found no significant correlation between such behavior and circulating testosterone levels (Wang et al., 2017). Overall, ENA theory seems to provide a reasonable evolutionary account for why males exhibit conduct disorder to a greater degree than females. More research is needed, however, regarding any testosterone connection. At the present time, I believe that ENA theory warrants just two checkmarks for its explanation of sex differences in conduct disorder.

3.11 Variable 11: Participation in the Paid Workforce, USD-Male

Sex differences in the amount of time spent working in the paid workforce has been widely investigated. As shown in Table 1, 116 studies of adults were located, all but 4 of which concluded that males surpassed females in the amount of time spent working for pay or profit. The four exceptions all reported no significant sex differences. Samples for these studies were derived from forty different countries along with twenty multinational studies.

3.11.1 Social Role Theory

Social role theory can draw on the fact that only females bear offspring to help account for greater males participate in the paid workforce. Thus, at least in the case of females with children, particularly those who breastfeed their infants, the likelihood of interruptions in workforce participation would be enhanced. Supporting this reasoning, substantial research has indicated that females are more intermittent in their paid workforce participation than are males (review: Ellis et al., 2024c, p. 651).

Another way that social role theory can account for sex differences in participation in the paid workforce involves men's greater physical strength. This sex difference would qualify men for a wider range of jobs than would be available to women. For example, strenuous manual labor, such as work in construction and the manipulation of heavy equipment, would be open to greater proportions of men than women. Research supporting this line of reasoning has come from studies comparing sex differences in occupational diversity, all indicating that jobs filled by males substantially surpass those filled by females (review: Ellis et al., 2024c, p. 674). Overall, social role theory explains sex differences in time spent in the paid workforce rather well, warranting it receiving three checkmarks in Table 1.

3.11.2 ENA Theory

The explanation offered by ENA theory for why males are more likely than females to be involved in paid workforce can be addressed in both evolutionary and neurohormonal terms. Regarding evolution, the theory's assertion that females bias their mating choices in favor of males with resources means that males who focus greater time and energy on obtaining resources will often have a reproductive edge over other males (Booth et al., 2000; Ellis, 2001; Pawłowski, 2000).

In the case of ENA theory's neurohormonal component, time spent in the paid workforce should be positively correlated with brain exposure to testosterone. No direct empirical evidence pertaining to this hypothesis was found. As a result, ENA theory receives two checkmarks beside this variable in Table 1.

3.12 Variable 12: Risk-Taking, USD-Male

Substantial research has assessed sex differences in risk-taking tendencies. Out of the 109 studies of adults that were located, 104 concluded that males are more prone toward risk-taking than are females. The five exceptions simply found no significant differences. Studies were based on samples from fourteen different countries along with two multinational studies.

3.12.1 Social Role Theory

The ability of social role theory to explain why risk-taking behavior is a USD would require assuming that risk-taking is promoted by physical strength. To test this assumption, one could seek to determine if, even *within* each sex, physical strength and risk-taking are positively correlated. Two studies that were located indicated that such a positive intra-sex correlation exists (Ball et al., 2010; Cho & Ahn 2020). Since this evidence is limited to confirming just one hypothesis, I gave two checkmarks to social role theory for explaining sex differences in risk-taking.

3.12.2 ENA Theory

The evolutionary component of ENA theory would offer the following reasoning about risk-taking: Such behavior could have evolved because it can often promote successful resource provisioning, and when males succeed in this regard, they increase their chances of attracting mates and thereby passing genes on to subsequent generations (Kruger et al., 2007). In other words, because females have evolved tendencies to prefer mates with resources (see Variable 13), risk-taking should be more pronounced in males than in females.

Regarding physiological underpinnings for risk-taking, ENA theory asserts that exposing the brain to testosterone should be central. Considerable evidence supports this assertion, both in terms of prenatal and postpubertal testosterone.

Concerning prenatal testosterone, most of the research comes from studies of the 2D:4D finger length ratio. Despite the crudeness of this indicator, I found nine pertinent studies, all of which indicated that high prenatal testosterone exposure is associated with greater risk-taking tendencies later in life (Aycinena et al., 2014; Brañas-Garza et al., 2018; Coates et al., 2009; Evans & Hampson, 2014; Finley et al., 2022; Manning, Bundred et al., 2003; Ronay & von Hippel, 2010b; Stenstrom et al., 2011; Vermeersch et al., 2008).

Turning to postpubertal circulating testosterone, which can be measured directly from the blood or saliva, studies also support the hypothesis of a positive correlation between brain exposure to this hormone and people's tendencies to take risks (Dariotis et al., 2016; Votinov et al., 2022; reviews: Apicella et al., 2015; Kurath & Mata, 2018). Overall, substantial scientific research supports ENA theory's explanation for why risk-taking is more common among males than females. For this reason, I gave this theory three checkmarks in Table 1 for explaining sex differences in risk-taking.

3.13 Variable 13: Preferring Mates with Resources, USD-Female

What are men and women looking for when they seek or choose mates? The only criterion for which our book located more than 100 findings was that of preferring mates with an ability to make a comfortable living. Specifically, 107 such studies were located. As shown in Table 1, all but three of these studies concluded that females consider this criterion to be of greater importance to them than was the case for males. The three exceptions simply concluded that the differences were not statistically significant. Twenty-seven countries were sampled along with twelve other multicountry studies.

3.13.1 Social Role Theory

Social role theory can be used to explain this sex difference in mate preferences by noting that only females are capable of bearing children and, once born, children benefit from receiving substantial parental care (often including breastmilk, which only females can provide). One way to test this explanation for why females are more interested than males are in a mate's ability to make a living involves females being stereotyped as the primary caregiver to children. Sex role theorists could then attribute the universality of this stereotype to the fact that only females can bear offspring (and breastfeed them after birth). One way to test this rather circular theoretical argument would be to study heterosexual women who intend to have children to those who do not intend to have children. If social role theory is correct, women who intend to remain childless should be less interested in marrying a man with the ability to make a comfortable living than would women intending to have children. Unfortunately, I could find no research bearing on this hypothesis. Therefore. just one checkmark was assigned to social role theory for potentially explaining this universal sex difference.

3.13.2 ENA Theory

The evolutionary component of ENA theory argues that, because only females can bear offspring and breastfeed them during infancy, they will have been favored for preferring mates with the ability to provide for them and their offspring throughout the offspring's childhood (Bereczkei & Voros, 1997;

Buss, 1988; Ellis, 2001; Zhu & Chang, 2019). In other words, under most conditions, women who choose males who seem capable of being a "good provider" will leave more offspring in future generations than women whose mate choices prioritize other mate characteristics (Brooks et al., 2022).

At the physiological level, ENA theory makes two predicts pertaining to sex differences in preferences for mates. First, it predicts that *low* brain exposure to testosterone will be associated with preferring mates with resources. No evidence directly bearing on this hypothesis was found.

The second prediction is that individuals with relatively high testosterone exposure will be better at accessing resources than those with low testosterone levels. This should even hold true within each sex. As noted earlier regarding Variable 1, considerable evidence supports this prediction, especially regarding postpubertal testosterone. Specifically, four studies of men have all concluded that income was positively correlated with circulating testosterone levels (Coates & Herbert, 2008; Harrison et al., 2021; Hughes & Kumari, 2019; Luoto, Krama et al., 2021). Evidence regarding prenatal testosterone also points toward a positive correlation (Nye et al., 2014; Gielen et al., 2016). Overall, I have assigned three checkmarks to ENA theory for its ability to account for sex differences in the tendency to prefer mates with resources.

3.14 Variable 14: Majoring in the Physical Sciences or Engineering, USD-Male

One can see in Table 1 that 102 studies of sex differences in people's tendencies to major in (or at least take advanced courses in) the physical sciences or engineering were found. All but four of these studies concluded that males surpass females in this regard. The exceptions all reported no significant sex differences and pertained specifically to the field of chemistry. Samples for these studies came from eleven different countries in addition to five multinational studies.

3.14.1 Social Role Theory

According to social role theory, sex differences in occupational interests, and thereby in academic areas of study, are the result of sex role socialization (Eccles, 1994). This idea would lead one to expect considerable cultural variability in the interests expressed by males and females when it comes to choosing college majors. Instead, our review of the literature indicated that, except for chemistry, considerably higher proportions of males select the physical sciences or engineering as majors in all countries that have been sampled. Overall, social role theory offers no explanation for this universal sex difference, leading me to assign it an "x" in Table 1.

3.14.2 ENA Theory

From an evolutionary perspective, female tendencies to prefer mates who can provide them and their offspring with resources should motivate males to take up a wider diversity of occupations that is true for females. Accordingly, ENA theory would predict that males would be more likely females to develop interests in many occupations having nothing to do with rearing offspring or even people in general. Obviously, the physical sciences and engineering often fit such a description. Evidence supporting such reasoning includes research showing that when males are compared to females, males (a) are more interested in things rather than people (Ellis et al., 2024b, pp. 868–871), (b) are better at spatial reasoning, especially regarding mental rotation (Ellis et al., 2024b, pp. 261–267), and (c) have a greater probability of being on the autism spectrum (Ellis et al., 2024b, pp. 656–657).

If ENA theory is correct, these three sex differences evolved to help males to comply with female preferences for competent resource procuring mates. Furthermore, the theory predicts that sex differences greater interest in things than in people are promoted by exposing the brain to male-typical levels of testosterone. Nevertheless, extreme testosterone exposure appears to sometimes result in what is known as the autism spectrum disorder (Baron-Cohen et al., 2006). Among the evidence that supports this deduction is that indicating that brain exposure to testosterone promotes interests in things, spatial reasoning ability, and autism (Ellis et al., 2024d, pp. 388–406, 461–463; Greenberg et al., 2018).

Furthermore, given the relatively high incomes associated with physical science and engineering occupations, ENA theory would hypothesize that individuals entering these professions will often be attractive to females. This is despite the fact that some males end up being exposed to such high levels of testosterone that they risk suffering from the autistic spectrum disorder (Cohen-Bendahan et al. 2005; Greenberg et al., 2018), ADHD, and extreme antisocial disorder (see especially the information on Variable 15 next).

Overall, tending to major in the physical sciences and engineering in college are more common among males than females in all countries studied. However, I was unable to find direct evidence linking testosterone to these tendencies. Therefore, I have given ENA theory just two checkmarks in Table 1.

3.15 Variable 15: Homicide, USD-Male

The last variable for which at least 100 studies were located involves homicidal behavior. As shown in Table 1, 101 findings were found, all of which concluded that males are more likely than females to perpetrate this type of crime.

Evidence in this regard was based on official data drawn from twenty-five different countries plus twenty-two additional studies of two or more countries.

3.15.1 Social Role Theory

Social role theory has already been discussed regarding two other crime-related variables: self-reported criminality (Variable 3) and official criminality in general (Variable 4). In neither case did social role theory seem to provide anything beyond weak explanations for why these general criminality measures would be more prevalent among males than among females. However, given that nearly all forms of homicide can be considered inherently violent, social role theory can predict that males would be more likely than females to engage in this type of offending.

The explanation would be as follows: Eagly and Wood (2012, p. 465) have argued that because of men's greater strength, they are more confident in their abilities to intimidate rivals and to win in aggressive encounters than are females. Consequently, social role theory predicts that homicide, as well as other violent crimes, should be more prevalent among males.

Supporting this prediction, one study indicated that, among males, muscularity is positively correlated with involvement in violent crime (Maddan et al., 2008) although another study reached the opposite conclusion (Beckley et al., 2014). Overall, since social role theory has at least some empirical support, I have given it two checkmarks beside Variable 15 in Table 1.

3.15.2 ENA Theory

The ENA theory offers both an evolutionary and a physiological explanation for why most murderers are males. As already noted, ENA theory postulates that males have been favored for being more competitive, aggressive, and inclined to take risks, thereby increasing their chances of obtaining resources with which to attract mates (Ellis, 2005). Violence can be seen as a frequent expression of extreme competitiveness, aggression, and risk-taking (Wilson & Daly, 1985; Villarreal, 2002). Accordingly, one can predict that males would have evolved all three of these tendencies more than females. While there are some exceptions depending on species and circumstances surrounding the violence, humans appear to share this sex difference with nearly all other mammals (Ellis et al., 2024c, pp. 371–374). In other words, in nearly all species of mammals, males are more violent than females. This suggests that evolutionary reasoning, rather than cultural sex role training, offers a more parsimonious explanation for sex differences in violence, with homicide being an especially extreme expression of violence.

The neurohormonal component of ENA theory asserts that brain exposure to testosterone contributes to physical violence (Ellis & Hoskin, 2015; Johnson & Thayer, 2016). Much of this contribution seems to involve testosterone's ability to alter the brain in ways that enhance an individual's motivation to be competitive and take risks (Casto & Edwards, 2016; Ronay & Von Hippel, 2010). Other testosterone influences seem to promote a lowered sensitivity to the pain caused to others (Vongas & Al Hajj, 2015; Zhuo et al., 2022). Regarding the latter point, nearly all studies have indicated that males are less empathetic than females (review: Ellis et al., 2024b, pp. 170–172).

It is also worth mentioning that while social role theory asserts that physical strength helps to promote physical aggression (Eagly & Wood 2012, p. 465), it does not explain *why* such a relationship would exist. The ENA theory does offer an explanation. Specifically, it indicates that testosterone not only affects brain functioning but also impacts other parts of the body, including muscularity and physical strength (Bhasin, Woodhouse et al. 2001; Sipilä et al., 2013). This difference between social role theory and ENA theory means that the latter is more vulnerable to refutation, which is, of course, a good feature in scientific theorizing (Archibald, 1967).

So, is there support for ENA theory regarding testosterone exposure being responsible for *both* physical strength and physical aggression? At least three lines of evidence point toward an affirmative answer. First, within both sexes, testosterone appears to promote violent behavior (Mhillaj et al., 2015; Pfaff, 2002; Swerdloff et al., 1992). Second, even within each sex, most research has indicated that *both* prenatal and postpubertal testosterone levels are positively correlated with aggression and violence (review: Ellis et al., 2019, 351–355). Third, regarding murderers specifically, three studies have concluded that they have higher average levels of testosterone than do males in general (Alnourani et al., 2017; Delgado et al., 2020; McAndrew, 2009). Given the weight of the this evidence, I have given ENA theory three checkmarks in Table 1 for its ability to explain the universal tendency for males to commit more homicides than females.

4 Discussion

This Element was written with three objectives in mind: First, it sought to highlight evidence that fifteen cognitive or behavioral variables can now be considered culturally universal when it comes to sex differences. Using a criterion of at least 100 studies from multiple countries, these fifteen variables can now be nearly certain to be USDs. The list of these appears in Table 1 along with other summary information regarding the actual number of studies, the number of countries sampled, and the existence of collaborating literature reviews and meta-analyses.

Second, this Element describes two theories that offer scientifically testable explanations for why USDs *would* exist in cognitive and behavioral traits. A summary of both theories appears in Figures 2 and 3.

Social role theory argues that sex differences in cognition and behavior are learned as part of each culture's socialization process. This means that males and females learn early in life what sex category they belong to and then learn to tailor their thinking and behavior accordingly. This learning may occur consciously or unconsciously and is usually unique to each individual's culture in terms of how rigorous the sex role training is. However, because of three biological sex differences (i.e., males being taller and stronger, and only females being able to bear offspring), some USDs in cognition and behavior will be found.

It is also worth adding that social role theory may help to explain why sex differences exist *between* countries and why these differences change over time (see Ellis et al., 2024c, pp. 1037–1099). Nevertheless, throughout this Element, the entire focus has been on sex differences that appear to exist in all societies, not the many more instances in which cognitive and behavioral sex differences are not found to be universal.

Turning to ENA theory, it can be conceptualized as having two interrelated parts. One part focuses on *why* (or "ultimate causes"), while the other addressed the question of *how* (or "proximate causes"). Regarding *why*, ENA theory argues that males and females have been sexually selected for their abilities to leave genes in subsequent generations. To accomplish this, males have evolved genes (primarily on the Y chromosome) that divert their would-be ovaries to become testes instead. In simple terms, this genetic transformation results in males producing substantially higher amounts of a sex hormone known as *testosterone*. While this hormone is produced by both sexes, the average developmental regimen in testosterone production is quite different from the regimen found in females (see Figure 1).

In evolutionary terms, ENA theory argues that females have evolved tendencies to be most sexually attracted to males who appear to be competent resource provisioners. As a result, the average male has evolved the tendency to produce high (male-typical) levels of testosterone. This elevated testosterone not only helps to promote greater strength and height (Giofre et al., 2025) but also increases male motivation to compete and take risks. Greater testosterone production also appears to promote tendencies to reason in spatial and nonsocial terms, thereby giving males occupational interests and abilities that often make males appealing to females (i.e., stable incomes). One should also note that

ENA theory asserts that testosterone can also have undesirable effects on cognition and behavior (e.g., greater ADHD, autism, and criminality traits).

The third reason for writing this Element was to provide an assessment of the explanatory power of both theories regarding each one of the fifteen nearly certain USDs. In other words, now that fifteen USDs have been identified for the first time (see Ellis et al., 2024d), it is possible to begin evaluating how well social role theory and ENA theory can explain why each USD is found in all human societies.

Of course, scientific theories tend to be complex and sometimes also vague or ambiguous. Therefore, they are not always easy to evaluate in terms of what is known as *predictive power*, a concept that essentially refers to the number of accurate predictions or explanation that the theory offers (Braithwaite, 1953; Cleland, 2011). In other words, if one has two theories designed to explain the same phenomena – in this case, USDs in cognition and behavior – the "best theory" is the one that accurately explains (or predicts) the greatest number of empirical observations.

4.1 Key Differences between Social Role Theory and ENA Theory

Both social role theory and ENA theory have been in the scientific domain for over two decades, and, of course, both theories are primarily designed to explain sex differences in traits. They differ, however, in terms of their focus. While social role theory attempts to explain average sex differences *regardless* of whether they are found to be the same in all cultures, ENA theory is largely confined to explaining sex differences that are culturally universal. Obviously, the only way to empirically test how well both theories account for USDs is to first identify at least some of these differences.

As shown in Figures 2 and 3, social role theory and ENA theory make substantially different assumptions. Four assumptions can be delineated. One of the most consequential differences involves the brain. Social role theory makes no assumptions of a neurological nature, while ENA theory assumes that male and female brains *must* differ on average, especially in terms of how they function. Considerable evidence supports ENA theory on this point, although there is also considerable overlap in nearly all respects (review: Ellis et al., 2024a, pp. 330–474).

A second difference is that ENA theory argues that sex differences in brain functioning are largely due to differential exposure to testosterone (and sometimes its metabolites). In other words, social role theory contends that the only biological factors responsible for USDs in cognition and behavior involve height, strength, and the ability to bear offspring; neurological sex differences are never mentioned.

A third difference between social role theory and ENA theory involves making comparisons acrost species. The ENA theory assumes that many, if not most, universal cognitive and behavioral sex differences will have parallels in many other species. While little attention was given to this possibility here, three examples include Variable 3 (involving performing indoor household chores), Variable 8 (holding elected political office), and Variable 15 (pertaining to the commission of homicide and other violent crimes). Social role theory would dismiss cognitive and behavioral sex differences that seem to be found in both humans and other animals as largely coincidences.

A fourth difference between social role theory and ENA theory involves hormones. While recent versions of social role theory have included the concept of "hormone regulation" (see Figure 2), it is treated as resulting from "socially constructed sex roles" without providing any testable details about how hormone regulations might produce sex differences in cognition or behavior. Nowhere does social role theory entertain the possibility that brain exposure to testosterone (especially *prenatal* testosterone) has any effects on cognitive and behavioral sex differences. In contrast, ENA theory is very specific in this regard. It asserts that sex differences in brain exposure to testosterone is essential for understanding why males and females often think and behave differently.

4.2 The Explanatory Power of Social Role Theory and ENA Theory

The last two columns of Table 1 provide a summary of my assessment of the relative explanatory power of both theories for each one of the fifteen nearly certain USDs. The concept of *explanatory power* refers to the ability of scientific theories to offer reasonable explanations for empirical observations and then go on to predict addition observations.

As summarily shown in Table 2, ENA theory seems to have greater explanatory power than social role theory for eight of the USDs, while social role theory was superior for explaining just two USDs. Regarding the existence of at least some independent empirical support, seven favored ENA theory, while just four favored social role theory. Beyond these differences, social role theory offered reasonable arguments for why six USDs should exist, although no supportive evidence could be found. In the case of the ENA theory, at least some independent empirical support was found for all its explanatory proposals.

Table 2 shows that four USDs were located for which social role theory offered no explanation, identified with an "x." These had to do with USDs in (a) performing routine household chores, (b) having ADHDs, (c) exhibiting

Table 2 Summary of the assessed explanatory power of social role theory and ENA theory

Explanatory Power Tally	Social Role Theory	Evolutionary Neuro-androgenic Theory
Substantial independent empirical support (✓✓✓)	2	8
Some independent empirical support (✓✓)	2	7
Argumentative plausibility but no independent empirical support located (✓)	7	0
Theoretical silence (x)	4	0
Total number of nearly certain USDs	15	15

conduct disorder, and (d) majoring in the physical sciences and engineering. Some supportive evidence was found for ENA theory in all but four of the fifteen USDs.

Both social role theory and ENA theory have been advocated in the scientific literature for over two decades. Nevertheless, assessing their explanatory power regarding USDs has had to wait until USDs have been identified. The book by three colleagues and myself led to the identification of fifteen variables for which the evidence of universality in sex difference is very high. Consequently, it seems reasonable to now seek to theoretically understand why such USDs would exist.

Parenthetically, another edition of this book is underway with 2034 as its targeted publication date. This book should help to uncover many more nearly certain USDs than the fifteen variables identified here. Any readers who might be interest in helping with this undertaking may contact any one of the book's four authors.

4.3 Limitations

Two limitations are worth recognizing regarding the evidence summarized throughout this Element. First, the approach that I have taken involves assuming that cultural universality can be estimated by counting the number of countries sampled and then comparing those results to findings reported by published literature reviews and meta-analyses. Obviously, the concept of *cultures* and *countries* are not identical. Basically, *cultures* refer to groups of people who usually share a common ethnicity, language, values, and traditions (Licht et al., 2007; Song, 2009). Especially in today's WEIRD countries, very few can be seen as even approximating a single identifiable culture. Therefore, the approach taken here – that of identifying and counting each country in which sex differences were found – can only be considered a rough approximation of *cultural universality*.

Second, findings reviewed in this Element should not be interpreted as indicating that sociocultural factors are unimportant regarding sex differences in cognition and behavior. To illustrate this point, nearly all studies have indicated that, throughout the world, more males than females hold elected political office (review: Ellis et al. 2024c, pp. 699–700, also see the discussion of Variable 8 in Table 1). Nevertheless, in recent decades, significant gains in the proportion of females serving in elected political office appear to have occurred (review: Ellis et al., 2024c, p. 701). These trends are almost certainly the result of sociocultural factors, such as some countries instituting laws requiring greater gender equality in election outcomes (Krook & Norris, 2014; Schwindt-Bayer, 2009). One country (i.e., France) in fact has attained a legislative sex ratio of 47.5 percent female after enacting a so-called *parity law* (Squires & Wickham-Jones, 2001). The point being made here is that social role theory may override ENA theory when it comes to explaining how sex differences can sometimes change over time due to sociocultural factors. However, for explaining cognitive and behavioral sex differences that are truly universal, ENA theory seems to have a substantial explanatory advantage.

5 Conclusions

Are there worldwide similarities in sex differences in how people think and behave, or are all sex differences unique to each culture? Based on evidence summarized in a recent book (Ellis et al., 2024d, pp. 814–823), fifteen cognitive and behavioral traits meet rigorous criteria for being universally different according to sex. This Element provides an assessment of how well two theories – social role theory and ENA theory – can explain why each one of these fifteen sex differences would exist.

In assessing the explanatory power of these two theories, it is useful to keep in mind that both theories have similarities as well as differences. Regarding similarities, both theories recognize that nearly all human thought and behavior is learned and that the learning processes occur throughout life within complex sociocultural contexts. Another similarity is that both theories recognize that adult males are larger and stronger on average and that only females can give birth. Otherwise, the two theories diverge especially regarding the importance of evolution and neurohormonal variables (Luxen, 2007).

Social role theory attributes USDs in cognitive and behavioral traits to the fact that males are taller and stronger plus the fact that only females can bear offspring. For sex differences that are *not* found in all cultures, social role theory leads one to expect wide diversities in cognitive and behavioral sex differences. As more studies of sex differences in cognition and behavior accumulate in the scientific literature, it should be possible to detect patterns that are predicted by social role theory in this regard.

The ENA theory, on the other hand, envisions complex neurohormonal factors as having evolved to affect many aspects of sex differences in cognitive and behavioral traits in similar ways throughout the world. Many of these differences should have evolved around the concept of *female choice* (Ellis, 2001), a concept referring to the reproductive advantage accrued to females who gravitate toward mating with males who are likely to provide a reliable supply of resources to the female and the offspring she and he jointly produce. After making this basic evolutionary assumption, ENA theory stipulates that neurohormonal factors, particularly involving testosterone, have evolved to help males comply with (and/or sometimes circumvent) female preferences for resource-procuring mates.

Although there are aspects of both theories that are difficult to test, the present review indicates that when it comes to explaining cognitive and behavioral USDs, more evidence currently supports ENA theory than social role theory. In particular, the neurohormonal component of ENA theory offers many testable hypotheses bearing on how the fifteen USDs should be associated with brain exposure to testosterone (Ellis, 2011; Hooven, 2021; Luxen, 2007, p. 385). As my coverage of Table 1 documents, several of these hypotheses already have considerable empirical support.

All scientific statements should be considered tentative, thereby reminding their supporters to remain open to eventual modification or even rejection as new evidence accumulates. In this regard, many more universal cognitive and behavioral sex differences may be found. In the fourth volume of our book, my three colleagues and I set the minimum number of supportive studies at ten (with no exceptions) in order to justify referring to them as "likely" USDs. This resulted in our identifying 275 likely USDs (Ellis et al., 2024d). In the future, as more studies are located, it is almost certain that many more sex differences will become apparent no matter what minimal criteria are set for their being recognized as USDs.

Let me to close on two tangential notes. First, a religious explanation for sex differences cannot be ignored. Such an explanation comes down to attributing sex differences to the will of God. While no serious attention was given to the God-made-us-that-way proposal here, my colleagues and I did consider it throughout the final volume of our book (Ellis et al., 2024d). In essence, despite its popularity among people at large, we found this explanation of USDs to be very difficult to empirically test.

Second, artificial intelligence (AI) may usure in new ways of identifying USDs that are even more objective and useful than those utilized here. As AI becomes increasingly capable of "reading" and interpreting scientific research reports, it may one day double or even triple the number of findings on sex differences summarized in our book (see Sohail et al., 2023; Wagner et al., 2022). Artificial intelligence could even assist scientists in improving the explanatory power of theories of sex differences. For AI to have the greatest beneficial effects in the field of sex difference research, its developers should keep in mind at least three distinctions. They are (a) *stereotypes* regarding sex differences, (b) people's desires for gender equality (or *in*equality in some cases), and (c) actual empirical *evidence* of sex differences (Marinucci et al., 2023; Nag & Yalçın, 2020). To ensure that these distinctions are maintained, elsewhere I have recommended that scientific documentation of research be made considerably more precise than is currently being done (Ellis, 2022a, 2022b).

References

Akkuş, M., & Avşar, P. A. (2024). 2D:4D ratio, alexithymia, impulsivity, aggression, and ADHD in men with opioid and methamphetamine use disorders: A comparative analysis with healthy controls. *Early Human Development, 189*,105946.

Aleman, A., Bronk, E., Kessels, R. P., Koppeschaar, H. P., & van Honk, J. (2004). A single administration of testosterone improves visuospatial ability in young women. *Psychoneuroendocrinology, 29*, 612–617.

Alnourani, A., Osman, A., & Alsheikh, A. (2017). Testosterone and homicide (An African perspective). *International Journal of Mental Health Psychiatry 3(2)*, 1–5. https://doi.org/10.4172/2471, 4372.

Angelov, N. & Karimi, A. (2012). Mothers' income recovery after childbearing, *Working Paper, No. 2012:20, Institute for Evaluation of Labour Market and Education Policy (IFAU)*. Uppsala, Sweden.

Apicella, C. L., Carré, J. M., & Dreber, A. (2015). Testosterone and economic risk taking: A review. *Adaptive Human Behavior and Physiology, 1*, 358–385.

Apicella, C. L., Dreber, A., Gray, P. B., et al. (2011). Androgens and competitiveness in men. *Journal of Neuroscience, Psychology, and Economics, 4*, 54–67.

Archer, J. (2019). The reality and evolutionary significance of human psychological sex differences. *Biological Reviews, 94*, 1381–1415.

Archibald, G. C. (1967). Refutation or comparison? *British Journal for the Philosophy of Science, 17*, 279–296.

Arnocky, S., Albert, G., Carré, J. M., & Ortiz, T. L. (2018). Intrasexual competition mediates the relationship between men's testosterone and mate retention behavior. *Physiology & Behavior, 186*, 73–78.

Asherson, P. (2005). Clinical assessment and treatment of attention deficit hyperactivity disorder in adults. *Expert review of neurotherapeutics, 5*(4), 525–539.

Auyeung, B., Knickmeyer, R., Ashwin, E., et al. (2012). Effects of fetal testosterone on visuospatial ability. *Archives of Sexual Behavior, 41*, 571–581.

Auyeung, B., Lombardo, M. V., & Baron-Cohen, S. (2013). Prenatal and postnatal hormone effects on the human brain and cognition. *European Journal of Physiology, 465*, 557–571.

Auyeung, T. W., Lee, J. S. W., Kwok, T., et al. (2011). Testosterone but not estradiol level is positively related to muscle strength and physical performance independent of muscle mass: A cross-sectional study in 1489 older men. *European Journal of Endocrinology, 164*, 811–817.

Aycinena, D., Baltaduonis, R., & Rentschler, L. (2014). Risk preferences and prenatal exposure to sex hormones for ladinos. *PLoS One*, *9*, e103332.

Babinski L. M., Hartshough C. S., Lambert N. M. (2001). A comparison of self-report of criminal involvement and official arrest records. *Aggressive Behavior*, *27*, 44–54.

Baker, M. D., & Maner, J. K. (2008). Risk-taking as a situationally sensitive male mating strategy. *Evolution and Human Behavior*, *29*, 391–395.

Ball, S., Eckel, C. C., & Heracleous, M. (2010). Risk aversion and physical prowess: Prediction, choice, and bias. *Journal of Risk and Uncertainty*, *41*, 167–193.

Barack, D. L., Ludwig, V. U., Parodi, F., et al. (2022). Attention deficits linked with proclivity to explore while foraging. *Proceedings of the Royal Society B: Biological Sciences*, https://doi.org/10.31234/osf.io/nyvjq.

Baron-Cohen, S., Lutchmaya, S., & Knickmeyer, R. (2006). *Prenatal testosterone in mind: Amniotic fluid studies*. Cambridge, MA: MIT Press.

Batalova, J. A., & Cohen, P. N. (2002). Premarital cohabitation and housework: Couples in cross-national perspective. *Journal of Marriage & the Family*, *64*, 743–755.

Beckley, A. L., Kuja-Halkola, R., Lundholm, L., Långström, N., & Frisell, T. (2014). Association of height and violent criminality: Results from a Swedish total population study. *International Journal of Epidemiology*, *43*, 835–842.

Beltz, A. M., Swanson, J. L., & Berenbaum, S. A. (2011). Gendered occupational interests: Prenatal androgen effects on psychological orientation to Things versus People. *Hormones and Behavior*, *60*, 313–317.

Bereczkei, T., Voros, S., Gal, A., & Bernath, L. (1997). Resources, attractiveness, family commitment: Reproductive decisions in human mate choice. *Ethology*, *103*, 681–699.

Berenbaum, S. A., Korman, K., & Leveroni, C. (1995). Early hormones and sex differences in cognitive abilities. *Learning and Individual Differences*, *7*, 303–321.

Bernhardt, I. (1994). Comparative advantage in self-employment and paid work. *Canadian Journal of Economics*, *27*, 273–289.

Bhasin, S., Woodhouse, L., Casaburi, R., et al. (2001). Testosterone dose-response relationships in healthy young men. *American Journal of Physiology-Endocrinology and Metabolism*, *281*, E1172–E1181.

Bijleveld, E., & Baalbergen, J. (2017). Prenatal exposure to testosterone (2D:4D) and social hierarchy together predict voice behavior in bankers. *PLoS One*, *12*, e0180008.

Blair, R. H., & Tucker, B. W. (1941). Nest sanitation. *British Birds*, *34*, 206–215, 226–235, 250–255.

Bönte, W., Procher, V. D., Urbig, D., & Voracek, M. (2017). Digit ratio (2D:4D) predicts self-reported measures of general competitiveness, but not behavior in economic experiments. *Frontiers in Behavioral Neuroscience*, *11*, 238, 1–17.

Booth, A., Carver, K., & Granger, D. A. (2000). Biosocial perspectives on the family. *Journal of Marriage and Family*, *62*, 1018–1034.

Braithwaite, R. B. (1953). *Scientific explanation a study of the function of theroy, probability and law in science*. Cambridge: CUP Archive.

Brañas-Garza, P., Galizzi, M. M., & Nieboer, J. (2018). Experimental and self-reported measures of risk taking and digit ratio (2D:4D): Evidence from a large, systematic study. *International Economic Review*, *59*, 1131–1157.

Breuning, L. G. (2018). Stimulating dopamine, serotonin, oxytocin, and endorphin by learning how they are stimulated in animals. *Journal of Medical and Clinical Research Review*, *2*, 1–3.

Brooks, R., Blake, K., & Fromhage, L. (2022). Effects of gender inequality and income inequality on within-sex mating competition under hypergyny. *Evolution and Human Behavior*, *43*, 501–509. https://doi.org/10.1016/j.evolhumbehav.2022.1008.1006.

Browne, K. R. (2006). Evolved sex differences and occupational segregation. *Journal of Organizational Behavior*, *27*, 143–162.

Buriticá-Marín, E. D., Daza-Arana, J. E., Jaramillo-Losada, J., Riascos-Zuñiga, A. R., & Ordoñez-Mora, L. T. (2023). Effects of a physical exercise program on the physical capacities of older adults: A quasi-experimental study. *Clinical Interventions in Aging*, 273–282.

Buss, D. M. (1988). The evolution of human intrasexual competition: Tactics of mate attraction. *Journal of Personality and Social Psychology*, *54*, 616–628.

Buss, D. M. (1989). Sex differences in human mate preferences: Evolutionary hypotheses testing in 37 cultures. *Behavioral and Brain Sciences*, *12*, 1–49.

Buss, D. M. (2007). The evolution of human mating. *Acta Psychologica Sinica*, *39*, 502–512.

Buss, D. M., & Schmitt, D. P. (1993). Sexual strategies theory: An evolutionary perspective on human mating. *Psychological Review*, *100*, 204–232.

Buss, D. M., & Schmitt, D. P. (2017). Sexual strategies theory: An evolutionary perspective on human mating. In *Interpersonal development* (pp. 297–325). London: Routledge.

Bussey, K., & Bandura, A. (1999). Social cognitive theory of gender development and differentiation. *Psychological Review*, *106*, 676–688.

Bütikofer, A., Figlio, D. N., Karbownik, K., Kuzawa, C. W., & Salvanes, K. G. (2019). Evidence that prenatal testosterone transfer from male twins reduces the fertility and socioeconomic success of their female co-twins. *Proceedings of the National Academy of Sciences*, *116*, 6749–6753.

Camara, B., Padoin, C., & Bolea, B. (2022). Relationship between sex hormones, reproductive stages and ADHD: A systematic review. *Archives of Women's Mental Health, 25*, 1–8.

Campbell, B. C., Dreber, A., Apicella, C. L., et al. (2010). Testosterone exposure, dopaminergic reward, and sensation-seeking in young men. *Physiology & Behavior, 99*, 451–456.

Cashdan, E. (1995). Hormones, sex, and status in women. *Hormones and Behavior, 29*, 354–366.

Casto, K. V., & Edwards, D. A. (2016). Testosterone, cortisol, and human competition. *Hormones and Behavior, 82*, 21–37.

Cebrián, I., & Moreno, G. (2015). The effects of gender differences in career interruptions on the gender wage gap in Spain. *Feminist Economics, 21*, 1–27.

Celec, P., Ostatníková, D., & Hodosy, J. (2015). On the effects of testosterone on brain behavioral functions. *Frontiers in Neuroscience, 9*, 12–25.

Cheng, J. T., & Tracy, J. L. (2014). Toward a unified science of hierarchy: Dominance and prestige are two fundamental pathways to human social rank. In J. T. Cheng & J. L. Tracy (Eds.), *The psychology of social status* (pp. 3–27). New York: Springer.

Charlesworth, B. (1991). The evolution of sex chromosomes. *Science, 251* (4997), 1030–1033.

Cho, E. K., & Ahn, H.-K. (2020). Muscling my way to my positive future: Physical exertion of strength and preference for risk. *Asia Marketing Journal, 22*, 27–39.

Cleland, C. E. (2011). Prediction and explanation in historical natural science. *The British Journal for the Philosophy of Science, 62*(3), 551–582.

Clutton-Brock, T. H., & Vincent, A. C. J. (1991). Sexual selection and the potential reproductive rates of males and females. Nature, *351*, 58–60.

Coates, J. M., & Herbert, J. (2008). Endogenous steroids and financial risk taking on a London trading floor. *Proceedings of the National Academy of Science, 105*, 6167–6172.

Coates, J. M., Gurnell, M., & Rustichini, A. (2009). Second-to-fourth digit ratio predicts success among high-frequency financial traders. *Proceedings of the National Academy of Sciences, 106*, 623–628.

Cohen-Bendahan, C. C., Van De Beek, C., & Berenbaum, S. A. (2005). Prenatal sex hormone effects on child and adult sex-typed behavior: Methods and findings. *Neuroscience & Biobehavioral Reviews, 29*, 353–384.

Cordain, L., Gotshall, R. W., & Eaton, S. B. (1998). Physical activity, energy expenditure and fitness: An evolutionary perspective. *International Journal of Sports Medicine, 19*, 328–335.

Covington, S. S., & Bloom, B. E. (2003). Gendered justice: Women in the Criminal Justice System. In B. E. Bloom (Ed.), *Gendered justice: Addressing female offenders* (pp. 1–20). Durham, NC: Carolina Academic Press.

Cutler, N. E., & Harootyan, R. (1975). Demography of the aged. In D. Woodruff & J. E. Birren (Eds.), *Aging: Scientific perspectives and social issues.* New York: Van Nostrand.

Dabbs, J. M., & Dabbs, M. G. (2000). *Heroes, rogues, and lovers: Testosterone and behavior.* New York: McGraw-Hill.

Dabbs, J. M., La Rue, D., & Williams, P. M. (1990). Testosterone and occupational choice: Actors, ministers, and other men. *Journal of Personality and Social Psychology, 59*, 1261–1265.

Daly, M. (2017). *Killing the competition: Economic inequality and homicide.* London: Routledge.

Dariotis, J. K., Schen, F. R., & Granger, D. A. (2016). Latent trait testosterone among 18-24-year-olds: Methodological considerations and risk associations. *Psychoneuroendocrinology, 67*, 1–9.

Darwin, C. (1871). *The descent of man, and selection in relation to sex.* London: John Murray.

Davis, E. P., & Pfaff, D. (2014). Sexually dimorphic responses to early adversity: implications for affective problems and autism spectrum disorder. *Psychoneuroendocrinology, 49*, 11–25.

Davis, J. T. M., & Hines, M. (2020). How large are gender differences in toy preferences? A systematic review and meta-analysis of toy preference research. *Archives of Sexual Behavior, 49*, 373–394.

Dawkins, R. (2006). *The selfish gene, with a new introduction by the author.* London: Oxford University Press.

de Bruin, I., Verheij, F., MA, T. W., & Ferdinand, R. F. (2006). Differences in finger length ratio between males with autism, pervasive developmental disorder-not otherwise specified, ADHD, and anxiety disorders. *Developmental Medicine & Child Neurology, 48*, 962–965.

De Jonge, F. H., Eerland, M. J., & Van De Poll, N. E. (1986). The influence of estrogen, testosterone and progesterone on partner preference, receptivity and proceptivity. *Physiology & behavior, 37*(6), 885–891.

Del Giudice, M. (2023). Ideological bias in the psychology of sex and gender. In C. L. Frisby, R. E. Redding, W. T. O'Donohue, & S. O. Lilienfeld (Eds.), *Ideological and political bias in psychology: Nature, scope, and solutions* (pp. 743–778). New York: Springer.

Delgado, P. F., Maya-Rosero, E., Franco, M., Montoya-Oviedo, N., Guatibonza, R., & Mockus, I. (2020). Testosterone and homicide: Neuroendocrine aspects of aggression. *Revista de la Facultad de Medicina, 68*, 283–294.

de Quinto, A., L. Hospido, & C. Sanz. (2021). The child penalty: Evidence from Spain. *Journal of the Spanish Economic Association, 12*, 585–606.

Dixson, A. F. (2009). *Sexual selection and the origins of human mating systems.* New York: Oxford University Press.

Eagly, A. H. (1987). *Sex differences in social behavior: A social-role interpretation.* Hillsdale, NJ: Erlbaum.

Eagly, A. H. (1997). Sex differences in social behavior: Comparing social role theory and evolutionary psychology. *American Psychologist, 52*, 1380–1383.

Eagly, A. H., & Wood, W. (1991). Explaining sex differences in social behavior: A meta-analytic perspective. *Personality and Social Psychology Bulletin, 17*, 306–315.

Eagly, A. H., & Wood, W. (1999). The origins of sex differences in human behavior: Evolved dispositions versus social role. *American Psychologist, 54*, 408–423.

Eagly, A. H., & Wood, W. (2005). Universal sex differences across patriarchal cultures ≠ evolved psychological dispositions. *Behavioral and Brain Sciences, 28*, 281–283.

Eagly, A. H., & Wood, W. (2012). Social role theory. *Handbook of theories of social psychology, 2*, 458–476.

Eagly, A. H., & Wood, W. (2013). The nature–nurture debates: 25 years of challenges in understanding the psychology of gender. *Perspectives on Psychological Science, 8*, 340–357.

Eagly, A. H., Wood, W., & Diekman, A. B. (2000). Social role theory of sex differences and similarities: A current appraisal. *The Developmental Social Psychology of Gender, 12*(174), 123–173.

Eccles J. S. (1994). Understanding women's educational and occupational choices: Applying the Eccles et al. model of achievement-related choices. *Psychology of Women Quarterly, 18*, 585–609.

Ecuyer-Dab, I., & Robert, M. (2004). Have sex differences in spatial ability evolved from male competition for mating and female concern for survival? *Cognition, 91*, 221–257.

Eisenegger, C., Kumsta, R., Naef, M., Gromoll, J., & Heinrichs, M. (2017). Testosterone and androgen receptor gene polymorphism are associated with confidence and competitiveness in men. *Hormones and Behavior, 92*, 93–102.

Eler, N. (2018). The correlation between right hand finger ratio (2D:4D) and the parameters of anthropometric and physical fitness in children. *Journal of Human Sciences, 15*, 656–664.

Ellis, L. (1994). The high and the mighty among man and beast: How universal is the relationship between height (or body size) and social status? In L. Ellis (Ed.), *Social stratification and socioeconomic inequality, volume 2: Reproductive and interpersonal aspects of dominance and status* (pp. 93–112). Westport, CT: Praeger.

Ellis, L. (2001). The biosocial female choice theory of social stratification. *Social Biology, 48*, 297–319.

Ellis, L. (2003). Genes, criminality, and the evolutionary neuroandrogenic theory. In A. Walsh & L. Ellis (Eds.), *Biosocial criminology: Challenging environmentalism's supremacy* (pp. 13–34). Hauppauge, NY: Nova Science.

Ellis, L. (2005). A theory explaining biological correlates of criminality. *European Journal of Criminology, 2*, 287–315.

Ellis, L. (2006). Gender differences in smiling: An evolutionary neuroandrogenic theory. *Physiology & Behavior, 88*, 303–308.

Ellis, L. (2011). Evolutionary neuroandrogenic theory and universal gender differences in cognition and behavior. *Sex Roles, 64*, 707–722.

Ellis, L. (2022a). Improving scientific communication by altering citation and referencing methods. *Journal of Social Science Studies, 9*(1), 1–13.

Ellis, L. (2022b). Citing without referencing and two other ways to reduce errors in scientific communication. *Journal of Methods and Measurement in the Social Sciences, 13*, 70–79.

Ellis, L., Hershberger, S., Field, E., et al. (2008). *Sex differences: Summarizing more than a century of scientific research*. New York: Psychology Press.

Ellis, L., & Hoskin, A. W. (2015). The evolutionary neuroandrogenic theory of criminal behavior expanded. *Aggression and Violent Behavior, 24*, 61–74.

Ellis, L., Hoskin, A. W., & Ratnasingam, M. (2018). *Handbook of social status correlates*. Amsterdam: Elsevier.

Ellis, L., Farrington, D. P., & Hoskin, A. W. (2019). *Handbook of crime correlates*, 2nd ed. San Diego, CA: Academic Press.

Ellis, L., Palmer, C. T., Hopcroft, R., & Hoskin, A. W. (2024a). *The handbook of sex differences Volume I Basic biology*. London: Taylor & Francis.

Ellis, L., Palmer, C. T., Hopcroft, R., & Hoskin, A. W. (2024b). *The handbook of sex differences Volume II Cognitive variables*. London: Taylor & Francis.

Ellis, L., Palmer, C. T., Hopcroft, R., & Hoskin, A. W. (2024c). *The handbook of sex differences Volume III Behavioral variables*. London: Taylor & Francis.

Ellis, L., Palmer, C. T., Hopcroft, R., & Hoskin, A. W. (2024d). *The handbook of sex differences Volume IV Identifying universal sex differences*. London: Taylor & Francis.

England, P. (2005). Gender inequality in labor markets: The role of motherhood and segregation. *Social Politics: International Studies in Gender, State & Society, 12*, 264–288.

Evans, K. L., & Hampson, E. (2014). Does risk-taking mediate the relationship between testosterone and decision-making on the Iowa Gambling Task? *Personality and Individual Differences*, *61*, 57–62.

Evertsson, M. (2014). Gender ideology and the sharing of housework and child care in Sweden. *Journal of Family Issues*, *35*, 927–949.

Fairchild, G., Hawes, D. J., Frick, P. J., et al. (2019). Conduct disorder. *Nature Reviews Disease Primers*, *5*(1), 43.

Fales, M. R., Frederick, D. A., Garcia, J. R., et al. (2016). Mating markets and bargaining hands: Mate preferences for attractiveness and resources in two national US studies. *Personality and Individual Differences*, *88*, 78–87.

Fausto-Sterling, A. (1992). *Myths of gender: Biological theories about women and men*. New York: Basic Books.

Finley, B., Kalwij, A., & Kapteyn, A. (2022). Born to be wild: Second-to-fourth digit length ratio and risk preferences. *Economics & Human Biology*, *47*, 101178.

Fisher, R. A. (1930). *The genetical theory of natural selection*. Oxford: Clarendon Press.

Fromonteil, S., Marie-Orleach, L., Winkler, L., & Janicke, T. (2023). Sexual selection in females and the evolution of polyandry. *PLoS Biology*, *21*(1), e3001916.

Galiano, V., Solazzo, G., Rabinovici, J., et al. (2021). Cord blood androgen levels of females from same sex and opposite sex twins–A pilot study. *Clinical Endocrinology*, *94*, 85–89.

Gao, K., & Tian, Z. (2022). The effect of motherhood on wages: Are women's wage penalties due to lack of career aspirations? *Applied Economics*, https://doi.org/10.1080/00036846.2022.2156469.

Garcia-Mainar, I., Montuenga, V. M., & García-Martín, G. (2018). Occupational prestige and gender-occupational segregation. *Work, employment and society*, *32*, 348–367.

Geary, D. C. (2019). Evolutionary perspective on sex differences in the expression of neurological diseases. *Progress in Neurobiology*, *176*, 33–53.

Geary, D. C. (2021). *Male, female: The evolution of human sex differences*, 3rd ed. Washington, DC: American Psychological Association.

Geher, G., & Kaufman, S. B. (2013). *Mating intelligence unleashed: The role of the mind in sex, dating, and love*. Oxford: Oxford University Press.

Giammanco, M., Tabacchi, G., Giammanco, S., Di Majo, D., & La Guardia, M. (2005). Testosterone and aggressiveness. *Medical Science Monitor*, *11*, 136–145.

Gielen, A. C., Holmes, J., & Myers, C. (2016). Prenatal testosterone and the earnings of men and women. *Journal of Human Resources*, *51*, 30–61.

Giofre, D, Geary, D. C., & Halsey, L. G. (2025). The sexy and formidable male body: Men's height and weight are condition dependent sexually selected traits. *Biology Letters*, *21*, 20240565.

Gooren, L. (2007). Testosterone and the brain. *Journal of Men's Health & Gender*, *4*, 344–351.

Gouchie, C., & Kimura, D. (1991). The relationship between testosterone levels and cognitive ability patterns. *Psychoneuroendocrinology*, *16*, 323–334.

Grant, V. J., & France, J. T. (2001). Dominance and testosterone in women. *Biological Psychology*, *58*, 41–47.

Greenberg, D. N., Warrier, V., Allison, C., and Baron-Cohen, S. (2018). Testing the empathizing-systemizing theory of sex differences and the extreme male brain theory of autism in half a million people. *Proceedings of the National Academy of Sciences*, *115*, 12152–12157.

Grimshaw, G. M., Bryden, M. P., & Finegan, J.-A. K. (1995). Relations between prenatal testosterone and cerebral lateralization in children. *Neuropsychology*, *9*, 68–81.

Griskevicius, V., Tybur, J. M., Gangestad, S. W., et al. (2009). Aggress to impress: hostility as an evolved context-dependent strategy. *Journal of Personality and Social Psychology*, *96*(5), 980–991.

Guigueno, M. F., & Sealy, S. G. (2012). Nest sanitation in passerine birds: Implications for egg rejection in hosts of brood parasites. *Journal of Ornithology*, *153*, 35–52.

Halpern, D. F. (2000). *Sex differences in cognitive abilities*. New York: Psychology Press.

Hankin, B. L. (2013). Critical reflections on evolutionary psychology and sexual selection theory as explanatory account of emergence of sex differences in psychopathology: Comment on Martel (2013). *Psychological Bulletin*, *138*, 1260–1264.

Harrison, S., Davies, N. M., Howe, L. D., & Hughes, A. (2021). Testosterone and socioeconomic position: Mendelian randomization in 306,248 men and women in UK Biobank. *Science Advances*, *7*(31), 8257.

Haynes, E., & DeBeliso, M. (2019). The relationship between cross fit performance and grip strength. *Turkish Journal of Kinesiology*, *5*, 15–21.

Heinsohn, R., & Double, M. C. (2004). Cooperate or speciate: New theory for the distribution of passerine birds. *Trends in Ecology & Evolution*, *19*, 55–57.

Helle, S., Laaksonen, T., Adamsson, A., Paranko, J., & Huitu, O. (2008). Female field voles with high testosterone and glucose levels produce male-biased litters. *Animal Behaviour*, *75*, 1031–1039.

Henriques-Neto, D. M., Peralta, M., & Marques, A. (2023). Puberty: Neurologic and physiologic development and its multifaceted dimensions. *Frontiers in Endocrinology, 14*, 1258656.

Herbert, J. (2015). *Testosterone: Sex, power, and the will to win* Oxford: Oxford Univeristy Press.

Hier, D. B., & Crowley Jr, W. F. (1982). Spatial ability in androgen-deficient men. *New England Journal of Medicine, 306*, 1202–1205.

Hines, M. (2005). *Brain gender.* New York: Oxford University Press

Hirschberg, A. L., Knutsson, J. E., Helge, T., et al. (2020). Effects of moderately increased testosterone concentration on physical performance in young women: A double blind, randomised, placebo-controlled study. *British Journal of Sports Medicine, 54*, 599–604.

Hoffman, B. F. (1977). Two new cases of XYY chromosome complement. *Canadian Psychiatric Association Journal, 22*, 447–455.

Hooven, C. (2021). *T: The story of testosterone, the hormone that dominates and divides us.* New York: Henry Holt.

Hooven, C. K., Chabris, C. F., Ellison, P. T., & Kosslyn, S. M. (2004). The relationship of male testosterone to components of mental rotation. *Neuropsychologia, 42*, 782–790.

Hoover, K. C. (2010). Smell with inspiration: The evolutionary significance of olfaction. *American Journal of Physical Anthropology, 143*, 63–74.

Horowitz, M., Yaworsky, W., & Kickham, K. (2014). Whither the blank slate? A report on the reception of evolutionary biological ideas among sociological theorists. *Sociological Spectrum, 34*, 489–509.

Hughes, A., & Kumari, M. (2019). Testosterone, risk, and socioeconomic position in British men: Exploring causal directionality. *Social Science & Medicine, 220*, 129–140.

Humphreys, L. G., Lubinski, D., & Yao, G. (1993). Utility of predicting group membership and the role of spatial visualization in becoming an engineer, physical scientist, or artist. *Journal of Applied Psychology, 78*, 250–261.

Huxley, J. (1942). *Evolution. The modern synthesis.* London: George Alien & Unwin.

Iannuzzi, V., Bacalini, M. G., Franceschi, C., & Giuliani, C. (2023). The role of genetics and epigenetics in sex differences in human survival. *Genus, 79*(1), 1–18.

Jacobs, L. F. (1996). Sexual selection and the brain. *Trends in Ecology & Evolution, 11*, 82–86.

Janicke, T., Häderer, I. K., Lajeunesse, M. J., & Anthes, N. (2016). Darwinian sex roles confirmed across the animal kingdom. *Science Advances, 2*, e1500983.

Janowsky, J. S., Oviatt, S. K., & Orwoll, E. (1994). Testosterone influences spatial cognition in older men. *Behavioral Neuroscience, 108*, 325–332.

Jardí, F., Laurent, M. R., Dubois, V., et al. (2018). Androgen and estrogen actions on male physical activity: A story beyond muscle. *Journal of Endocrinology, 238*, R31–R52.

Jarvinen, M., & Kannus, P. (1997). Current concepts review-injury of an extremity as a risk factor for the development of osteoporosis. *Journal of Bone and Joint Surgery, 79*, 263–276.

Jašarević, E., Geary, D. C., & Rosenfeld, C. S. (2012). Sexually selected traits: A fundamental framework for studies on behavioral epigenetics. *ILAR Journal, 53*, 253–269.

Jobling, M., & Tyler-Smith, C. (2019). *Human evolutionary genetics: Origins, peoples, and disease*: New York: Garland Science.

Johnson, D. D. P., & Thayer, B. A. (2016). The evolution of offensive realism: Survival under anarchy from the Pleistocene to the present. *Politics and the Life Sciences, 35*, 1–26.

Jonason, P. K. (2007). An evolutionary psychology perspective on sex differences in exercise behaviors and motivations. *Journal of Social Psychology, 147*, 5–14.

Jones, S. C., & Rossiter, J. R. (2009). Social and religious factors in adolescents' drug use. *Journal of Child & Adolescent Substance Abuse, 18*, 85–92.

Judge, T. A., & Cable, D. M. (2004). The effect of physical height on workplace success and income: preliminary test of a theoretical model. *Journal of Applied Psychology, 89*, 428–437.

Kanazawa, S. (2005). Is "discrimination" necessary to explain the sex gap in earnings? *Journal of Economic Psychology, 26*, 269–287.

Kang, J., Hense, J., Scheersoi, A., & Keinonen, T. (2019). Gender study on the relationships between science interest and future career perspectives. *International Journal of Science Education, 41*, 80–101.

Karimi, A. (2014). *Effects of the timing of births on women's earnings: Evidence from a natural experiment*. Working Paper, No. 2014:17, Institute for Evaluation of Labour Market and Education Policy (IFAU), Uppsala, Sweden.

Kaplan, H., Hill, K., Lancaster, J., & Hurtado, A. M. (2000). A theory of human life history evolution: Diet, intelligence, and longevity. *Evolutionary Anthropology: Issues, News, and Reviews, 9*, 156–185.

Keevil, B., MacDonald, P., Macdowall, W., et al. (2014). Salivary testosterone measurement by liquid chromatography tandem mass spectrometry in adult males and females. *Annals of Clinical Biochemistry, 51*, 368–378.

Kempel, P., Gohlke, B., Klempau, J., et al. (2005). Second-to-fourth digit length, testosterone, and spatial ability. *Intelligence, 33*, 215–230.

Key, C., & Ross, C. (1999). Sex differences in energy expenditure in non-human primates. *Proceedings of the Royal Society of London. Series B: Biological Sciences*, *266*(1437), 2479–2485.

Kimura, D. (2000). *Sex and cognition*. MIT Press.

Kimura, D., & Hampson, E. (1994). Cognitive pattern in men and women is influenced by fluctuations in sex hormones. *Current Directions in Psychological Science*, *3*, 57–61.

Kirillova, G. P., Vanyukov, M. M., Kirisci, L., & Reynolds, M. (2008). Physical maturation, peer environment, and the ontogenesis of substance use disorders. *Psychiatry Research*, *158*, 43–53.

Kleven, H., Landais, C., & Søgaard, J. E. (2019). Children and gender inequality: Evidence from Denmark. *American Economic Journal: Applied Economics*, *11*, 181–209.

Knickmeyer, R. C., & Baron-Cohen, S. (2006). Fetal testosterone and sex differences. *Early Human Development*, *82*, 755–760.

Kolakowski, D., & Malina, R. M. (1974). Spatial ability, throwing accuracy and man's hunting heritage. *Nature*, *251*, 410–412.

Kopsida, E., Stergiakouli, E., Lynn, P. M., Wilkinson, L. S., & Davies, W. (2009). The role of the Y chromosome in brain function. *Open Neuroendocrinology Journal*, *2*, 20–31.

Kordsmeyer, T. L., Hunt, J., Puts, D. A., Ostner, J., & Penke, L. (2018). The relative importance of intra-and intersexual selection on human male sexually dimorphic traits. *Evolution and Human Behavior*, *39*, 424–436.

Krook, M. L., & Norris, P. (2014). Beyond quotas: Strategies to promote gender equality in elected office. *Political Studies*, *62*, 2–20.

Kruger, D. J., Wang, X.-T., & Wilke, A. (2007). Towards the development of an evolutionarily valid domain-specific risk-taking scale. *Evolutionary Psychology*, *5*(3), 147470490700500306.

Kumagai, H., Yoshikawa, T., Zempo-Miyaki, A., et al. (2018). Vigorous physical activity is associated with regular aerobic exercise-induced increased serum testosterone levels in overweight/obese men. *Hormone and Metabolic Research*, *50*, 73–79.

Kurath, J., & Mata, R. (2018). Individual differences in risk taking and endogenous levels of testosterone, estradiol, and cortisol: A systematic literature search and three independent meta-analyses. *Neuroscience & Biobehavioral Reviews*, *90*, 428–446.

Kutschera, U., & Niklas, K. J. (2004). The modern theory of biological evolution: An expanded synthesis. *Naturwissenschaften*, *91*, 255–276.

Lachance-Grzela, M., & Bouchard, G. (2010). Why do women do the lion's share of housework? A decade of research. *Sex Roles*, *63*, 767–780.

Lemiere, J., Boets, B., & Danckaerts, M. (2010). No association between the 2D: 4D fetal testosterone marker and multidimensional attentional abilities in children with ADHD. *Developmental Medicine & Child Neurology, 52*, e202–e208.

Lennon, M. C. (1994). Women, work, and well-being: The importance of work conditions. *Journal of Health and Social Behavior, 35*, 235–247.

Lerner, D. A., Verheul, I., & Thurik, R. (2019). Entrepreneurship and attention deficit/hyperactivity disorder: A large-scale study involving the clinical condition of ADHD. *Small Business Economics, 53*, 381–392.

Liben, L. S., Susman, E. J., Finkelstein, J. W., et al. (2002). The effects of sex steroids on spatial performance: a review and an experimental clinical investigation. *Developmental Psychology, 38*, 236–253.

Licht, A. N., Goldschmidt, C., & Schwartz, S. H. (2007). Culture rules: The foundations of the rule of law and other norms of governance. *Journal of Comparative Economics, 35*, 659–688.

Liebenberg, L. (1990). *The Art of Tracking the Origin of Science*. Cape Town: David Phillip.

Lightfoot, J. T. (2008). Sex hormones' regulation of rodent physical activity: A review. *International Journal of Biological Sciences, 4*, 126–132.

Lippa, R. (1998). Gender-related individual differences and the structure of vocational interests: The importance of the people–things dimension. *Journal of Personality and Social Psychology, 74*, 996–1009.

Lippa, R. A. (2002). *Gender, nature, and nurture*. Mahwah, NJ: Lawrence Erlbaum Associates.

Lippa, R. A. (2009). Sex differences in sex drive, sociosexuality, and height across 53 nations: Testing evolutionary and social structural theories. *Archives of Sexual Behavior, 38*, 631–651.

Lippa, R. A. (2010). Sex differences in personality traits and gender-related occupational preferences across 53 nations: Testing evolutionary and social-environmental theories. *Archives of Sexual Behavior, 39*, 619–636.

Luoto, S., & Varella, M. A. C. (2021). Pandemic leadership: Sex differences and their evolutionary–developmental origins. *Frontiers in Psychology, 12*, 618–641.

Lüpold, S., Manier, M. K., Puniamoorthy, N., et al. (2016). How sexual selection can drive the evolution of costly sperm ornamentation. *Nature, 533* (7604), 535–538.

Luxen, M. F. (2007). Sex differences, evolutionary psychology, and biosocial theory: Biosocial theory is no alternative. *Theory & Psychology, 17*, 383–394.

Määttänen, I., Jokela, M., Hintsa, T., et al. (2013). Testosterone and temperament traits in men: Longitudinal analysis. *Psychoneuroendocrinology, 38*, 2243–2248.

Maddan, S., Walker, J. T., & Miller, J. M. (2008). Does size really matter? A reexamination of Sheldon's somatotypes and criminal behavior. *Social Science Journal*, *45*, 330–344.

Magnusson, C. (2009). Gender, occupational prestige, and wages: A test of devaluation theory. *European Sociological Review*, *25*, 87–101.

Majid, A., Speed, L., Croijmans, I., & Arshamian, A. (2017). What makes a better smeller? *Perception*, *46*, 406–430.

Manning, J. T., & Taylor, R. P. (2001). Second to fourth digit ratio and male ability in sport: implications for sexual selection in humans. *Evolution and Human Behavior*, *22*, 61–69.

Manning, J. T., Bundred, P. E., Newton, D. J., & Flanagan, B. F. (2003). The second to fourth digit ratio and variation in the androgen receptor gene. *Evolution and Human Behavior*, *24*, 399–405.

Marinucci, L., Mazzuca, C., & Gangemi, A. (2023). Exposing implicit biases and stereotypes in human and artificial intelligence: state of the art and challenges with a focus on gender. *AI & Society*, *38*, 747–761.

Marlowe, F. W. (2007). Hunting and gathering: The human sexual division of foraging labor. *Cross-Cultural Research*, *41*, 170–195.

Martel, M. M. (2013). Sexual selection and sex differences in the prevalence of childhood externalizing and adolescent internalizing disorders. *Psychological Bulletin*, *139*, 1221–1259.

Martel, M. M., Gobrogge, K. L., Breedlove, S. M., & Nigg, J. T. (2008). Masculinized finger-length ratios of boys, but not girls, are associated with attention-deficit/hyperactivity disorder. *Behavioral Neuroscience*, *122*, 273–285.

Maxfield, S., Shapiro, M., Gupta, V., & Hass, S. (2010). Gender and risk: Women, risk taking and risk aversion. *Gender in Management: An International Journal*, *25*, 586–604.

Maxwell, N. (1974). The rationality of scientific discovery part I: The traditional rationality problem. *Philosophy of Science*, *41*(2), 123–153.

Mazur, A., & Booth, A. (1998). Testosterone and dominance in men. *Behavioral and Brain Sciences*, *21*, 353–363.

McAndrew, F. T. (2009). The interacting roles of testosterone and challenges to status in human male aggression. *Aggression and Violent Behavior*, *14*, 330–335.

McFadden, D., Westhafer, J. G., Pasanen, E. G., Carlson, C. L., & Tucker, D. M. (2005). Physiological evidence of hypermasculinization in boys with the inattentive type of attention-deficit/hyperactivity disorder (ADHD). *Clinical Neuroscience Research*, *5*, 233–245.

Mead, M. (1935). *Sex and temperament in three primitive societies*. New York: Mentor Books.

Mead, M. (1949). *Male and female: A study of the sexes in a changing world.* Oxford: William Morrow.

Mealey, L. (2000). *Sex differences: Development and evolutionary strategies.* San Diego: Academic Press.

Mehta, P. H., Jones, A. C., & Josephs, R. A. (2008). The social endocrinology of dominance: basal testosterone predicts cortisol changes and behavior following victory and defeat. *Journal of Personality and Social Psychology, 94,* 1078–1092.

Mhillaj, E., Morgese, M. G., Tucci, P., et al. (2015). Effects of anabolic-androgens on brain reward function. *Frontiers in Neuroscience, 9,* 295–305.

Mikac, U., Buško, V., Sommer, W., & Hildebrandt, A. (2016). Analysis of different sources of measurement error in determining second-to-fourth digit ratio, a potential indicator of perinatal sex hormones exposure. *Review of Psychology, 23,* 39–49.

Miller, E. M. (1994). Prenatal sex hormone transfer: A reason to study opposite-sex twins. *Personality and Individual Differences, 17,* 511–529.

Millet, K., & Dewitte, S. (2008). A subordinate status position increases the present value of financial resources for low 2D:4D men. *American Journal of Human Biology, 20,* 110–115.

Miranda-Mendizabal, A., Castellví, P., Parés-Badell, O., et al. (2019). Gender differences in suicidal behavior in adolescents and young adults: systematic review and meta-analysis of longitudinal studies. *International Journal of Public Health, 64,* 265–283.

Modlinska, K., Adamczyk, D., Maison, D., & Pisula, W. (2020). Gender differences in attitudes to vegans/vegetarians and their food preferences, and their implications for promoting sustainable dietary patterns–a systematic review. *Sustainability, 12,* 6292.

Moffat, S. D., & Hampson, E. (1996). A curvilinear relationship between testosterone and spatial cognition in humans: Possible influence of hand preference. *Psychoneuroendocrinology, 21,* 323–337.

Moffit, D. M., & Swanik, C. B. (2011). The association between athleticism, prenatal testosterone, and finger length. *Journal of Strength & Conditioning Research, 25,* 1085–1088.

Moore, C. B., McIntyre, N. H., & Lanivich, S. E. (2021). ADHD-related neurodiversity and the entrepreneurial mindset. *Entrepreneurship Theory and Practice, 45,* 64–91.

Murphy, G. L., & Medin, D. L. (1985). The role of theories in conceptual coherence. *Psychological Review, 92,* 289–316.

Nag, P., & Yalçın, Ö. (2020). Gender stereotypes in virtual agents. *Proceedings of the 20th ACM International Conference on Intelligent Virtual Agents, 41,* https://doi.org/10.1145/3383652.3423876.

Neave, N., Laing, S., Fink, B., & Manning, J. T. (2003). Second to fourth digit ratio, testosterone, and perceived male dominance. *Proceedings of the Royal Society of London B: Biological Sciences, 270*(1529), 2167–2172.

Negri-Cesi, P., Colciago, A., Celotti, F., & Motta, M. (2004). Sexual differentiation of the brain: Role of testosterone and its active metabolites. *Journal of Endocrinological Investigation, 27,* 120–127.

Ngun, T. C., Ghahramani, N., Sánchez, F. J., Bocklandt, S., & Vilain, E. (2011). The genetics of sex differences in brain and behavior. *Frontiers in Neuroendocrinology, 32,* 227–246.

Nicolaou, N., Patel, P. C., & Wolfe, M. T. (2018). Testosterone and tendency to engage in self-employment. *Management Science, 64,* 1825–1841.

Nye, J. V., Yudkevich, M., Orel, E., & Kochergina, E. (2014). The effects of prenatal testosterone on adult wages: Evidence from Russian rims data and measured 2D:4D digit ratios. *Higher School of Economics Research Paper No. WP BRP, 71–84.*

O'Connor, S., & Liu, H. (2023). Gender bias perpetuation and mitigation in AI technologies: challenges and opportunities. *AI & Society, 38,* 1–13.

Okami, P., & Shackelford, T. K. (2001). Human sex differences in sexual psychology and behavior. *Annual Review of Sex Research, 12,* 186–241.

Parker, G. A. (1974). Courtship persistence and female-guarding as male time investment strategies. *Behaviour, 48,* 157–183.

Pawłowski, B. (2000). The biological meaning of preferences on the human mate market. *Przegląd Antropologiczny ñ Anthropological Review, 63,* 39–72.

Perret, M. (2018). Revisiting the Trivers-Willard theory on birth sex ratio bias: Role of paternal condition in a Malagasy primate. *PLoS One, 13*(12), e0209640.

Petersen, R. M., & Higham, J. P. (2020). The role of sexual selection in the evolution of facial displays in male non-human primates and men. *Adaptive Human Behavior and Physiology, 6,* 249–276.

Pettay, J. E., Helle, S., Jokela, J., & Lummaa, V. (2007). Natural selection on female life-history traits in relation to socio-economic class in pre-industrial human populations. *PLoS One, 2*(7), e606.

Pfaff, D. W. (2002). *Hormones, brain and behavior.* Amsterdam: Elsevier.

Pfaff, D. W., Rubin, R. T., Schneider, J. E., & Head, G. (2018). *Principles of hormone/behavior relations.* New York: Academic Press.

Pinker, S. (2002). *The blank slate: The modern denial of human nature.* New York: Viking.

Popper, K. (2013). *Realism and the aim of science: From the postscript to the logic of scientific discovery.* London: Routledge.

Preston, S. D. (2013). The origins of altruism in offspring care. *Psychological Bulletin, 139,* 1305–1318.

Puts, D. (2016). Human sexual selection. *Current Opinion in Psychology, 7,* 28–32.

Puts, D. A., Jones, B. C., & DeBruine, L. M. (2012). Sexual selection on human faces and voices. *Journal of Sex Research, 49,* 227–243.

Putz, T., & H. Engelhardt-Woelfler (2014). The effects of the first birth timing on women's wages: A longitudinal analysis based on the German socio-economic panel. *Zeitschrifte Fur Familienforschung-Journal of Family Research, 26,* 302–330.

Quinsey, V. L. (2002). Evolutionary theory and criminal behaviour. *Legal and Criminological Psychology, 7,* 1–13.

Ratnu, V. S., Emami, M. R., & Bredy, T. W. (2017). Genetic and epigenetic factors underlying sex differences in the regulation of gene expression in the brain. *Journal of Neuroscience Research, 95,* 301–310.

Riachy, R., McKinney, K., & Tuvdendorj, D. R. (2020). Various factors may modulate the effect of exercise on testosterone levels in men. *Journal of Functional Morphology and Kinesiology, 5,* 81–94.

Rismayanthi, C., Kristiyanto, A., & Doewes, M. (2022). Psychological-based physical exercise education model for improving elderly physical fitness. *International Journal of Education in Mathematics, Science and Technology, 10,* 162–174.

Roberts, B. A., & Martel, M. M. (2013). Prenatal testosterone and preschool disruptive behavior disorders. *Personality and Individual Differences, 55,* 962–966.

Roldan, E. R. S., & Gomendio, M. (1999). The Y chromosome as a battle ground for sexual selection. *Trends in Ecology & Evolution, 14,* 58–62.

Ronay, R., & Von Hippel, W. (2010). Power, testosterone, and risk-taking. *Journal of Behavioral Decision Making, 23,* 473–482.

Roney, J. R., & Simmons, Z. L. (2013). Hormonal predictors of sexual motivation in natural menstrual cycles. *Hormones and Behavior, 63,* 636–645.

Roof, R. L., & Havens, M. D. (1992). Testosterone improves maze performance and induces development of a male hippocampus in females. *Brain Research, 572,* 310–313.

Rowe, R., Maughan, B., Worthman, C. M., Costello, E. J., & Angold, A. (2004). Testosterone, antisocial behavior, and social dominance in boys:

Pubertal development and biosocial interaction. *Biological Psychiatry, 55,* 546–552.

Ryan, B. C., & Vandenbergh, J. G. (2002). Intrauterine position effects. *Neuroscience & Biobehavioral Reviews, 26,* 665–678.

Ryan, M. J. (2021). Darwin, sexual selection, and the brain. *Proceedings of the National Academy of Sciences, 118,* e2008194118.

Salk, R. H., Hyde, J. S., & Abramson, L. Y. (2017). Gender differences in depression in representative national samples: Meta-analyses of diagnoses and symptoms. *Psychological Bulletin, 143,* 783–822.

Sanderson, S. K., & Ellis, L. (1992). Theoretical and political perspectives of American sociologists in the 1990s. *American Sociologist, 23,* 26–42.

Sarkar, P., Bergman, K., Fisk, N., O'Connor, T., & Glover, V. (2007). Amniotic fluid testosterone: Relationship with cortisol and gestational age. *Clinical Endocrinology, 67,* 743–747.

Sarkar, P., Bergman, K., O'Connor, T. G., & Glover, V. (2008). Maternal antenatal anxiety and amniotic fluid cortisol and testosterone: possible implications for foetal programming. *Journal of neuroendocrinology, 20*(4), 489–496.

Savic, I., Frisen, L., Manzouri, A., Nordenstrom, A., & Lindén Hirschberg, A. (2017). Role of testosterone and Y chromosome genes for the masculinization of the human brain. *Human Brain Mapping, 38,* 1801–1814.

Schmitt, D. P. (2003). Universal sex differences in the desire for sexual variety: Tests from 52 nations, 6 continents, and 13 islands. *Journal of Personality and Social Psychology, 85,* 85–104.

Schmitt, D. P., Realo, A., Voracek, M., & Allik, J. (2008). Why can't a man be more like a woman? Sex differences in big five personality traits across 55 cultures. *Journal of Personality and Social Psychology, 94,* 168–182.

Schneck, S. (2020). Self-employment as a source of income inequality. *Eurasian Business Review, 10,* 45–64.

Schuett, W., Tregenza, T., & Dall, S. R. X. (2010). Sexual selection and animal personality. *Biological Reviews, 85,* 217–246.

Schwartz, S. H., & Rubel, T. (2005). Sex differences in value priorities: Cross-cultural and multimethod studies. *Journal of Personality and Social Psychology, 89,* 1010–1028.

Schwindt-Bayer, L. A. (2009). Making quotas work: The effect of gender quota laws on the election of women. *Legislative Studies Quarterly, 34,* 5–28.

Scott-Phillips, T. C., Dickins, T. E., & West, S. A. (2011). Evolutionary theory and the ultimate–proximate distinction in the human behavioral sciences. *Perspectives on Psychological Science, 6,* 38–47.

Silverman, I., Choi, J., & Peters, M. (2007). The hunter-gatherer theory of sex differences in spatial abilities: Data from 40 countries. *Archives of Sexual Behavior, 36*, 261–268.

Simmons, Z. L., & Roney, J. R. (2011). Variation in CAG repeat length of the androgen receptor gene predicts variables associated with intrasexual competitiveness in human males. *Hormones and Behavior, 60*, 306–312.

Sinervo, B., Miles, D. B., Frankino, W. A., Klukowski, M., & DeNardo, D. F. (2000). Testosterone, endurance, and Darwinian fitness: Natural and sexual selection on the physiological bases of alternative male behaviors in side-blotched lizards. *Hormones and Behavior, 38*, 222–233.

Sipilä, S., Narici, M., Kjaer, M., et al. (2013). Sex hormones and skeletal muscle weakness. *Biogerontology, 14*, 231–245.

Skutch, A. F. (1976). *Parent birds and their young*. Austin: University of Texas Press.

Smith, A. R., Chein, J., & Steinberg, L. (2013). Impact of socio-emotional context, brain development, and pubertal maturation on adolescent risk-taking. *Hormones and Behavior, 64*, 323–332.

Smith, E. A. (2004). Why do good hunters have higher reproductive success? *Human Nature, 15*, 343–364.

Smuts, B. (1995). The evolutionary origins of patriarchy. *Human nature, 6*(1), 1–32.

Sohail, S. S., Madsen, D. Ø., Himeur, Y., & Ashraf, M. (2023). Using ChatGPT to navigate ambivalent and contradictory research findings on artificial intelligence. *Frontiers in Artificial Intelligence, 6*, PMC10413582.

Soma, K. (2006). Testosterone and aggression: Berthold, birds and beyond. *Journal of Neuroendocrinology, 18*, 543–551.

Song, S. (2009). The subject of multiculturalism: Culture, religion, language, ethnicity, nationality, and race? In B. d. Bruin & C. F. Zurn (Eds.), *New waves in political philosophy* (pp. 177–197). New York: Springer.

Sorokowski, P., Karwowski, M., Misiak, M., et al. (2019). Sex differences in human olfaction: A meta-analysis. *Frontiers in Psychology, 10*, 242–251.

Souza, A. L., Conroy-Beam, D., & Buss, D. M. (2016). Mate preferences in Brazil: Evolved desires and cultural evolution over three decades. *Personality and Individual Differences, 95*, 45–49.

Squires, J., & Wickham-Jones, M. (2001). *Women in parliament: A comparative analysis*. Manchester: Equal Opportunities Commission.

Stearns, S. C. (1993). The evolutionary links between fixed and variable traits. *Acta Palaeontologica Polonica, 38*, 215–232.

Steinmetz, J., Bosak, J., Sczesny, S., & Eagly, A. H. (2014). Social role effects on gender stereotyping in Germany and Japan. *Asian Journal of Social Psychology, 17*, 52–60.

Stenstrom, E., Saad, G., Nepomuceno, M. V., & Mendenhall, Z. (2011). Testosterone and domain-specific risk: Digit ratios (2D: 4D and rel2) as predictors of recreational, financial, and social risk-taking behaviors. *Personality and Individual Differences, 51*, 412–416.

Stevenson, J. C., Everson, P. M., Williams, D. C., et al. (2007). Attention deficit/hyperactivity disorder (ADHD) symptoms and digit ratios in a college sample. *American Journal of Human Biology, 19*, 41–50.

Stockemer, D. (2011). Women's parliamentary representation in Africa: The impact of democracy and corruption on the number of female deputies in national parliaments. *Political Studies, 59*, 693–712.

Stoet, G., & Geary, D. C. (2020). Sex-specific academic ability and attitude patterns in students across developed countries. *Intelligence, 81*, 101453.

Storer, T. W., Woodhouse, L., Magliano, L., et al. (2008). Changes in muscle mass, muscle strength, and power but not physical function are related to testosterone dose in healthy older men. *Journal of the American Geriatrics Society, 56*, 1991–1999.

Swerdloff, R. S., Wang, C., Hines, M., & Gorski, R. (1992). Effect of androgens on the brain and other organs during development and aging. *Psychoneuroendocrinology, 17*, 375–383.

Talia, C., Raja, E.-A., Bhattacharya, S., & Fowler, P. A. (2020). Testing the twin testosterone transfer hypothesis – intergenerational analysis of 317 dizygotic twins born in Aberdeen, Scotland. *Human Reproduction, 35*, 1702–1711.

Tahira, A. C., Barbosa, A. R., Feltrin, A. S. A., et al. (2019). Putative contributions of the sex chromosome proteins SOX3 and SRY to neurodevelopmental disorders. *American Journal of Medical Genetics Part B: Neuropsychiatric Genetics, 180*, 390–414.

Tapp, A. L., Maybery, M. T., & Whitehouse, A. J. (2011). Evaluating the twin testosterone transfer hypothesis: A review of the empirical evidence. *Hormones and Behavior, 60*, 713–722.

Toivainen, T., Pannini, G., Papageorgiou, K. A., et al. (2018). Prenatal testosterone does not explain sex differences in spatial ability. *Scientific Reports, 8*, 13653.

Tosi, L. L., Boyan, B. D., & Boskey, A. L. (2005). Does sex matter in musculoskeletal health? The influence of sex and gender on musculoskeletal health. *Journal of Bone and Joint Surgery, 87*, 1631–1647.

Tremblay, R. E. (1998). Testosterone, physical aggression, dominance, and physical development in early adolescence. *International Journal of Behavioral Development, 22*, 753–777.

Trivers, R. L. (1972). Parental investment and sexual selection. In B. Campbell (Ed.), *Sexual selection and the descent of man, 1871–1971* (pp. 136–179). Chicago: Aldine-Atherton.

Trivers, R. L. (1976). Sexual selection and resource-accruing abilities in Anolis garmani. *Evolution, 30*, 253–269.

Turner, C., McClure, R., & Pirozzo, S. (2004). Injury and risk-taking behavior —a systematic review. *Accident Analysis & Prevention, 36*(1), 93–101.

Vaamonde, D., Da Silva-Grigoletto, M. E., García-Manso, J. M., Barrera, N., & Vaamonde-Lemos, R. (2012). Physically active men show better semen parameters and hormone values than sedentary men. *European Journal of Applied Physiology, 112*, 3267–3273.

Valla, J. M., & Ceci, S. J. (2011). Can sex differences in science be tied to the long reach of prenatal hormones? Brain organization theory, digit ratio (2D:4D), and sex differences in preferences and cognition. *Perspectives on Psychological Science, 6*, 134–146.

Van Goozen, S. H., Wiegant, V. M., Endert, E., Helmond, F. A., & Van de Poll, N. E. (1997). Psychoendocrinological assessment of the menstrual cycle: the relationship between hormones, sexuality, and mood. *Archives of sexual behavior, 26*, 359–382.

Vercken, E., Wellenreuther, M., Svensson, E. I., & Mauroy, B. (2012). Don't fall off the adaptation cliff: When asymmetrical fitness selects for suboptimal traits. *PLoS One, 7*(4), e34889.

Vermeersch, H., T'Sjoen, G., Kaufman, J., & Vincke, J. (2008). 2D:4D, sex steroid hormones and human psychological sex differences. *Hormones and Behavior, 54*, 340–346.

Villarreal, A. (2002). Political competition and violence in Mexico: Hierarchical social control in local patronage structures. *American Sociological Review, 67*, 477–498.

Volman, I., Toni, I., Verhagen, L., & Roelofs, K. (2011). Endogenous testosterone modulates prefrontal–amygdala connectivity during social emotional behavior. *Cerebral Cortex, 21*, 2282–2290.

Vongas, J. G., & Al Hajj, R. (2015). Competing sexes, power, and testosterone: How winning and losing affect people's empathic responses and what this means for organisations. *Applied Psychology, 64*, 308–337.

Votinov, M., Knyazeva, I., Habel, U., Konrad, K., & Puiu, A. A. (2022). A Bayesian modeling approach to examine the role of testosterone administration on the endowment effect and risk-taking. *Frontiers in Neuroscience, 16*, 858168.

Wagner, G., Lukyanenko, R., & Paré, G. (2022). Artificial intelligence and the conduct of literature reviews. *Journal of Information Technology, 37*, 209–226.

Wai, J., Lubinski, D., & Benbow, C. P. (2009). Spatial ability for STEM domains: Aligning over 50 years of cumulative psychological knowledge solidifies its importance. *Journal of Educational Psychology, 101*, 817–829.

Wang, L.-J., Chou, M.-C., Chou, W.-J., et al. (2017). Potential role of pre-and postnatal testosterone levels in attention-deficit/hyperactivity disorder: Is there a sex difference? *Neuropsychiatric Disease and Treatment, 13*, 1331–1343.

Waynforth, D. (2001). Mate choice trade-offs and women's preference for physically attractive men. *Human Nature, 12*, 207–219.

Weisfeld, G. E., & Dillon, L. M. (2012). Applying the dominance hierarchy model to pride and shame, and related behaviors. *Journal of Evolutionary Psychology, 10*, 15–41.

Welker, K. M., Gruber, J., & Mehta, P. H. (2015). A positive affective neuroendocrinology approach to reward and behavioral dysregulation. *Frontiers in Psychiatry, 6*, 93–105.

White, R. E., Thornhill, S., & Hampson, E. (2007). A biosocial model of entrepreneurship: The combined effects of nurture and nature. *Journal of Organizational Behavior, 28*, 451–466.

Wiederman, M. W. (1993). Evolved gender differences in mate preferences: Evidence from personal advertisements. *Ethology and Sociobiology, 14*, 331–351.

Wilson, M. I., & Daly, M. (1985). Competitiveness, risk taking, and violence: The young male syndrome. *Ethology and Sociobiology, 6*, 59–73.

Wilson, M. L., Miller, C. M., & Crouse, K. N. (2017). Humans as a model species for sexual selection research. *Proceedings of the Royal Society B: Biological Sciences, 284*(1866), 20171320.

Wilson, M., Daly, M., & Pound, N. (2009). Sex differences and intrasexual variation in competitive confrontation and risk taking: An evolutionary psychological perspective. In D. W. Pfaff, A. P. Arnold, A. M. Etgen, S. E. Fahrbach, & R. T. Rubin (Eds.), *Hormones, brain and behavior* (pp. 2825–2852). San Diego: Elsevier.

Witteveen, D., & Westerman, J. (2023). Structural change shapes career mobility opportunities: An analysis of cohorts, gender, and parental class. *Work, Employment and Society, 37*, 97–116.

Wong, B. B., & Candolin, U. (2005). How is female mate choice affected by male competition? *Biological Reviews, 80*, 559–571.

Wood, W., & Eagly, A. H. (2002). A cross-cultural analysis of the behavior of women and men: Implications for the origins of sex differences. *Psychological Bulletin, 128*, 699–727.

Wood, W., & Eagly, A. H. (2012). Biosocial construction of sex differences and similarities in behavior. In M. P. Zanna (Ed.), *Advances in Experimental Social Psychology* (Vol. 46, pp. 55–123). Amsterdam: Elsevier.

Wynn, T. G., Tierson, F. D., & Palmer, C. T. (1996). Evolution of sex differences in spatial cognition. *American Journal of Physical Anthropology, 101*(S23), 11–42.

Zaidi, Z. F. (2010). Gender differences in human brain: A review. *Open Anatomy Journal, 2*, 27–55.

Zeng, L.-N., Zong, Q.-Q., Yang, Y., et al. (2020). Gender difference in the prevalence of insomnia: A meta-analysis of observational studies. *Frontiers in Psychiatry, 11*, 577429.

Zhu, N., & Chang, L. (2019). Evolved but not fixed: A life history account of gender roles and gender inequality. *Frontiers in Psychology, 10*, 1709–1721.

Zhuo, S., Zhang, W., Fan, J., et al. (2022). Single-dose testosterone administration modulates instant empathic responses to others' pain: An EEG study. *Psychoneuroendocrinology, 141*, 105768.

Zitzmann, M. (2006). Testosterone and the brain. *Aging Male, 9*, 195–199.

Acknowledgments

Appreciation is extended to the following individuals for having made helpful suggestions for improving various drafts of this manuscript: Mark Horowitz, Anthony W. Hoskin, Alice H. Eagly, John T. Manning, Craig T. Palmer, Marco Del Giudice, and two anonymous reviewers. Despite modifying the manuscript substantially to accommodate their comments, I accept responsibility for any errors, oversights, and ambiguities that may appear in the final version.

Cambridge Elements

Applied Evolutionary Science

David F. Bjorklund
Florida Atlantic University

David F. Bjorklund is a Professor of Psychology at Florida Atlantic University in Boca Raton, Florida. He is the Editor-in-Chief of the *Journal of Experimental Child Psychology*, the Vice President of the Evolution Institute, and has written numerous articles and books on evolutionary developmental psychology, with a particular interest in the role of immaturity in evolution and development.

Editorial Board

David Buss, *University of Texas, Austin*
David Geary, *University of Missouri*
Mhairi Gibson, *University of Bristol*
Patricia Hawley, *Texas Tech University*
David Lancy, *Utah State University*
Jerome Lieberman, *Evolution Institute*
Todd Shackelford, *Oakland University*
Viviana Weeks-Shackelford, *Oakland University*
David Sloan Wilson, *SUNY Binghamton*
Nina Witoszek, *University of Oslo*
Rafael Wittek, *University of Groningen*

About the Series

This series presents original, concise, and authoritative reviews of key topics in applied evolutionary science. Highlighting how an evolutionary approach can be applied to real-world social issues, many Elements in this series will include findings from programs that have produced positive educational, social, economic, or behavioral benefits. Cambridge Elements in Applied Evolutionary Science is published in association with the Evolution Institute.

Cambridge Elements≡

Applied Evolutionary Science

Elements in the Series

Improving Breastfeeding Rates: Evolutionary Anthropological Insights for Public Health
Emily H. Emmott

The Hidden Talents Framework: Implications for Science, Policy, and Practice
Bruce J. Ellis, Laura S. Abrams, Ann S. Masten, Robert J. Sternberg, Nim Tottenham and Willem E. Frankenhuis

An Introduction to Positive Evolutionary Psychology
Glenn Geher, Megan Fritche, Avrey Goodwine, Julia Lombard, Kaitlyn Longo and Darcy Montana

Superorganism: Toward a New Social Contract for Our Endangered Species
Peter A. Corning

The Evolution of Reputation-Based Cooperation: A Goal Framing Theory of Gossip
Rafael Wittek and Francesca Giardini

Attachment and Parent-Offspring Conflict: Origins in Ancestral Contexts of Breastfeeding and Multiple Caregiving
Sybil L. Hart

The Evolved Mind and Modern Education: Status of Evolutionary Educational Psychology
David C. Geary

Evolutionary Perspectives on Enhancing the Quality of Life
Mads Larsen and Nina Witoszek

Evolution in International Relations
Jeremy Garlick

Evolution and the Fate of Humankind
Peter A. Corning

Strengths and Weaknesses of Two Theories for Explaining 15 Universal Sex Differences in Cognition and Behavior
Lee Ellis

A full series listing is available at: www.cambridge.org/EAES

Printed by Integrated Books International,
United States of America